Say

Right in

ITALIAN

**Easily Pronounced
Language Systems, Inc.**

Clyde Peters, Author

**Mc
Graw
Hill**

New York   Chicago   San Francisco   Lisbon   London   Madrid   Mexico City
Milan   New Delhi   San Juan   Seoul   Singapore   Sydney   Toronto

The *McGraw·Hill* Companies

Library of Congress Cataloging-in-Publication Data

Say it right in Italian / by Easily Pronounced Language Systems.
      p.   cm. — (Say it right)
   Includes index.
   ISBN 0-07-146917-6
    1. Italian language—Pronunciation.   I. Easily Pronounced Language
Systems.   II. Series.

PC1137.S39   2006
458.3'421—dc22   2005058364

6 7 8 9 10 11 12 13 14 15 16 17 18 19 20 21 22 23   FGR/FGR   0 9

ISBN 978-0-07-146917-3
MHID   0-07-146917-6

McGraw-Hill books are available at special quantity discounts to use as premiums
and sales promotions, or for use in corporate training programs. To contact a
representative please e-mail us at bulksales@mcgraw-hill.com.

Also available: *Say It Right in Arabic • Say It Right in Brazilian Portuguese • Say It
Right in Chinese • Say It Right in Chinese, Audio Edition • Say It Right in French • Say
It Right in French, Audio Edition • Say It Right in German • Say It Right in Italian • Say
It Right in Italian, Audio Edition • Say It Right in Japanese • Say It Right in Korean •
Say It Right in Russian • Say It Right in Spanish • Dígalo correctamente en inglés [Say
It Right in English]*

Author: Clyde Peters
Illustrations: Luc Nisset
President, EPLS Corporation: Betty Chapman, isayitright.com
Senior Series Editor: Priscilla Leal Bailey
Italian Consultant: Lucia Colazio

This book is printed on acid-free paper.

CONTENTS

INTRODUCTION

The SAY IT RIGHT FOREIGN LANGUAGE PHRASE BOOK SERIES has been developed with the conviction that learning to speak a foreign language should be fun and easy!

All SAY IT RIGHT phrase books feature the EPLS Vowel Symbol System, a revolutionary phonetic system that stresses consistency, clarity, and above all, simplicity!

Since this unique phonetic system is used in all SAY IT RIGHT phrase books, you only have to learn the VOWEL SYMBOL SYSTEM ONCE!

The SAY IT RIGHT series uses the easiest phrases possible for English speakers to pronounce and is designed to reflect how foreign languages are used by native speakers.

You will be amazed at how confidence in your pronunciation leads to an eagerness to talk to other people in their own language.

Whether you want to learn a new language for travel, education, business, study, or personal enrichment, SAY IT RIGHT phrase books offer a simple and effective method of pronunciation and communication.

PRONUNCIATION GUIDE

Most English speakers are familiar with the Italian word **Pizza**. This is how the correct pronunciation is represented in the EPLS Vowel Symbol System.

All Italian vowel sounds are assigned a specific non-changing symbol. When these symbols are used in conjunction with consonants and read normally, pronunciation of even the most difficult foreign word becomes incredibly EASY.

On the following page are all the EPLS Vowel Symbols used in this book. They are EASY to LEARN since their sounds are familiar. Beneath each symbol are three English words which contain the sound of the symbol.

Practice pronouncing the words under each symbol until you mentally associate the correct vowel sound with the correct symbol. Most symbols are pronounced the way they look!

THE SAME BASIC SYMBOLS ARE USED IN ALL SAY IT RIGHT PHRASE BOOKS!

EPLS VOWEL SYMBOL SYSTEM

Ⓐ

Ace
Bake
Safe

ⒺⒺ

See
Feet
Meet

Ⓘ

Ice
Kite
Pie

Ⓞ

Oak
Cold
Sold

ⓄⓄ

Cool
Pool
Too

ⓔ̆

Men
Red
Bed

ⓐⓗ

Mom
Hot
Off

ⓄⓌ

Cow
How
Now

EPLS CONSONANTS

Consonants are letters like **T**, **D**, and **K**. They are easy to recognize and their pronunciation seldom changes. The following EPLS pronunciation guide letters represent some unique Italian consonant sounds.

R   Represents a slightly rolled **r** sound.

R̲   Represents a strongly rolled **r** sound.

TS   Represents the letter **z** in Italian. Pronounce the word hi**ts** without the hi or simply say pi**zz**a! Listen closely to a native speaker to master this sound.

KY   Pronounce like the **c** in **c**ute.

CH   Pronounce like the **ch** in **ch**air.

PRONUNCIATION TIPS

- Each pronunciation guide word is broken into syllables. Read each word slowly, one syllable at a time, increasing speed as you become more familiar with the system.

- In Italian it is important to emphasize certain syllables. This mark (´) over the syllable reminds you to stress that syllable.

- This phrase book provides a means to speak and be understood in Italian. To perfect your Italian accent you must listen closely to Italian speakers and adjust your speech accordingly.

- The pronunciation and word choices in this book were chosen for their simplicity and effectiveness.

- **PF** or **PPC** are abbreviations for **per favore** or **per piacere** which means "please" in Italian. You will see these abbreviations throughout the book.

ICONS USED IN THIS BOOK

KEY WORDS

You will find this icon at the beginning of chapters indicating key words relating to chapter content. These are important words to become familiar with.

PHRASEMAKER

The Phrasemaker icon provides the traveler with a choice of phrases that allows the user to make his or her own sentences.

Say It Right in ITALIAN

ESSENTIAL WORDS AND PHRASES

Here are some basic words and phrases that will help you express your needs and feelings in Italian.

Hello

Buon giorno

BWON JOR-NO

How are you?

Come sta?

KO-ME ST-ah

Fine / Very well

Molto bene

MOL-TO BE-NE

And you?

E lei?

E LE-EE

Good-bye

Arrivederci

ah-REE-VE-DER-CHEE

Good morning

Buon giorno

BWŌN JŌR-NŌ

Good evening

Buona sera

BWŌ-Nah SĔ-Rah

Good night

Buona notte

BWŌ-Nah NŌT-Tĕ

Mr.

Signor

SĒN-YŌR

Mrs.

Signora

SĒN-YŌ-Rah

Miss

Signorina

SĒN-YŌ-RĒ-Nah

Yes

Sí

S**EE**

No

No

N**O**

Please

Per piacere / Per favore

P**E**R   P**EE**-**ah**-CH**E**-R**E**

P**E**R   F**ah**-V**O**-R**E**

Always remember to say **please** and **thank you**.

Thank you

Grazie

GR**ah**-TS**EE**-**E**

Excuse me

Mi scusi

M**EE**   SK**oo**-Z**EE**

I'm sorry

Mi dispiace

M**EE**   D**EE**S-P**EE**-**ah**-CH**E**

I'm a tourist.

Sono un turista.

SŌ-NO ⓄN Tᴏᴏ-RₑEˊS-Tₐₕ

I do not speak Italian.

Non parlo italiano.

NON PₐₕˊR-LO EE-Tₐₕ-LEE-ₐₕˊ-NO

I speak a little Italian.

Parlo un poco italiano.

PₐₕˊR-LO ᴏᴏN POˊ-KO
EE-Tₐₕ-LEE-ₐₕˊ-NO

Do you understand English?

Capisce l'inglese?

Kₐₕ-PEEˊ-SHₑ LEEN-GLₑˊ-Sₑ

I don't understand!

Non capisco!

NON Kₐₕ-PEEˊS-KO

Please repeat.

Ripeta, per favore.

REE-Pₑˊ-Tₐₕ Pₑʀ Fₐₕ-VOˊ-Rₑ

FEELINGS

I want...

Voglio...

VOͅL-YO...

I have...

Ho...

O...

I know.

Lo so.

LO SO

I don't know.

Non lo so.

NON LO SO

I like it.

Mi piace.

MEE PEE-ah-CHe

I don't like it.

Non mi piace.

NON MEE PEE-ah-CHe

I'm lost.

Mi sono perduto. (male) Mi sono perduta. (female)

MEE SÓ-NO PÉR-DOO-TO (ah)

I'm in a hurry.

Ho fretta.

O FRÉT-Tah

I'm tired.

Sono stanco. (male) Sono stanca. (female)

SÓ-NO STahN-KO (ah)

I'm ill.

Sono ammalato. (male) Sono ammalata. (female)

SÓ-NO ahM-MahL-Lah-TO (ah)

I'm hungry.

Ho fame.

O Fah-MEE

I'm thirsty.

Ho sete.

O SÉ-TEE

I'm angry.

Sono adirato.

SÓ-NO ah-DEE-Rah-TO

INTRODUCTIONS

My name is...

Mi chiamo...

MEE KEE-ah-MO...

What's your name?

Come si chiama?

KO-MEE SEE KEE-ah-Mah

Where are you from?

Di dov'è Lei?

DEE DO-VEE LEE-EE

Do you live here?

Lei abita qui?

LEE-EE ah-BEE-Tah KWEE

I just arrived.

Sono appena arrivato.

SO-NO ahP-PEE-Nah ah-BEE-Vah-TO

What hotel are you [staying] at?

In quale hotel sta?

EEN KWah-LEE O-TEEL STah

I'm at the...hotel.

Sono all' hotel...

SO´-NO ᵃʰL O-TᵉL...

It was nice to meet you.

È stato un piacere incontrarla.

ᵉ STᵃʰ-TO ᵒᵒN PEE-ᵃʰ-CHᵉ-Rᵉ
EEN-KON-TRᵃʰR-Lᵃʰ

See you tomorrow.

Ci vediamo domani.

CHEE Vᵉ-DEE-ᵃʰ-MO DO´-Mᵃʰ-NEE

See you next time.

Arrivederci a presto.

ᵃʰ-REE-Vᵉ-DᵉR-CHEE ᵃʰ PRᵉS-TO

See you later.

A più tardi.

ᵃʰ PEE-ᵒᵒ´ TᵃʰR-DEE

Good luck!

Buona fortuna!

BWO´-Nᵃʰ FOR-Tᵒᵒ´-Nᵃʰ

THE BIG QUESTIONS

Who?

Chi?

K**EE**

Who is it?

Chi è?

K**EE**   **ě**

What?

Cosa?

K**O**́-Z**ah**

What's that?

Che cos'è quello?

K**ě**   K**O**́-Z**ě**   KW**ě**́L-**l̵O**

When?

Quando?

KW**ah**́N-**D̵O**

Where?

Dove?

D**O**́-V**ě**

Where is...?

Dov'è...?

DO-Vé...

Which?

Quale?

KWah-Lé

Why?

Perchè?

PéR-Ké

How?

Come?

KO-Mé

How much? (does it cost)

Quanto costa?

KWahN-TO KOS-Tah

How long?

Per quanto tempo?

PéR KWahN-TO TéM-PO

ASKING FOR THINGS

The following phrases are valuable for directions, food, help, etc.

I would like...

Vorrei....

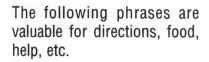

I need...

Ho bisogno di...

Ⓞ Bⓔⓔ-Z'Ⓞ'N-YⓄ Dⓔⓔ...

Can you...

Può...?

PWⓄ...

When asking for things be sure to say <u>please</u> and <u>thank you</u>.

Please	Thank you
Per piacere	Grazie
Pⓔ̈R Pⓔⓔ-ah-CHⓔ̈-Rⓔ̈	GRah-TSⓔⓔ-ⓔ̈

PHRASEMAKER

Combine **I would like** with the following phrases beneath, and you will have a good idea how to ask for things.

I would like...

Vorrei....

V⊙-Bё́-Œ... PPC

▸ **more coffee**

ancora del caffè

ⓐN-K⊙́-Bⓐ D̃ⓔL Kⓐ-F̃ё́

▸ **some water**

dell'acqua

D̃ⓔL Lⓐ́-KWⓐ

▸ **some ice**

del ghiaccio

D̃ⓔL GŒ-ⓐ́-CH⊙

▸ **the menu**

il menù

ŒL M̃ё̃-N⊚́

PHRASEMAKER

Here are a few sentences you can
use when you feel the urge to say
I need... or **Can you**...?

I need...
Ho bisogno...
Ⓞ Bⓔⓔ-ZⓄ́N-YⓄ....

▶ **help**
d'aiuto
DⒶ-Yⓞⓞ́-TⓄ

▶ **directions**
di indicazioni
Dⓔⓔ ⓔⓔN-Dⓔⓔ-KⒶ-TSⓔⓔ-Ó-Nⓔⓔ

▶ **more money**
di più soldi
Dⓔⓔ Pⓔⓔ-ⓞⓞ́ SⓄ́L-Dⓔⓔ

▶ **change**
di moneta
Dⓔⓔ MⓄ-Nⓔ̃́-TⒶ

▶ **a lawyer**
di un avvocato
Dⓔⓔ ⓞⓞN ⒶV-VⓄ-KⒶ́-TⓄ

PHRASEMAKER

Can you...

Può...

PW⓪...

▶ **help me?**

aiutarmi?

ⓐ-Y⓪⓪-Tⓐ'R-Mⓔⓔ

▶ **show me?**

indicarmi?

ⓔⓔN-Dⓔⓔ-Kⓐ'R-Mⓔⓔ

▶ **give me...?**

darmi...?

Dⓐ'R-Mⓔⓔ

▶ **tell me...?**

dirmi...?

Dⓔⓔ'R-Mⓔⓔ

▶ **take me to...?**

portarmi al...?

P⓪R-Tⓐ'R-Mⓔⓔ ⓐL...

ASKING THE WAY

No matter how independent you are, sooner or later you'll probably have to ask for directions.

Where is...?

Dov'è...?

DⓄ-Vⓔ́...

Is it near?

È vicino?

ⓔ́ VⒺⒺ-CHⒺⒺ-NⓄ

Is it far?

E lontano?

ⓔ́ LⓄN-Tⓐ́-NⓄ

I'm lost!

Mi sono perduto! (male)   Mi sono perduta! (female)

MⒺⒺ SⓄ́-NⓄ PⓔⓇ-DⓄⓄ́-TⓄ (ⓐ)

I'm looking for...

Sto cercando...

STⓄ CHⓔⓇ-Kⓐ́N-DⓄ...

PHRASEMAKER

Where is...

Dov'è...

DO-Vē...

▸ **the restroom?**

la toilette?

Lah TWah-Lēt

▸ **the telephone?**

il telefono?

EEL Tē-Lē-FO-NO

▸ **the beach?**

la spiaggia?

Lah SPEE-ah-Jah

▸ **the hotel...?**

l'hotel...?

LO-Tēl

▸ **the train for...?**

il treno per...?

EEL TRē-NO PēR...

TIME

What time is it?

Che ora è?

Kĕ Ō-Rah ĕ

Morning

Mattino

Mah-T-TĒĒ-NŌ

Noon

Mezzogiorno

Mĕ-TSŌ-JŌR-NŌ

Night

Notte

NŌT-Tĕ

Today

Oggi

Ō-JĒĒ

Tomorrow

Domani

DŌ-Mah-NĒĒ

This week

Questa settimana

KW@'S-T@ S@T-T@-M@-N@

This month

Questo mese

KW@'S-T@ M@'-S@

This year

Quest'anno

KW@'ST-@N-N@

Now

Adesso

@-D@'S-S@

Soon

Presto

PR@'S-T@

Later

Più tardi

P@-@' T@R-D@

Never

Mai

M@'-@

WHO IS IT?

I

Io

You (Formal)	**(Informal)**
Lei	Tu
L ĕ́-EE	T oo
Use this form of you with people you don't know well.	Use this form of you with people you know well.

We

Noi

N oy

They

Loro

LŌ-RŌ

THE, A (AN), AND SOME

To use the correct form of **The**, **A** (**An**), or **Some**, you must know if the Italian word is masculine or feminine. Often you will have to guess! If you make a mistake, you will still be understood.

The

Il, Lo, L'

ⒺⒺL / LⓄ / L

The before a singular masculine noun:
(il) man is handsome.

I, Gli

ⒺⒺ / LYⒺⒺ

The before a plural masculine noun:
(i) men are handsome.

La

LⒶⒽ

The before a singular feminine noun:
(la) woman is pretty.

I, Le

ⒺⒺ / LⒺ

The before a plural feminine noun:
(i) women are pretty.

A or An

Un / Uno

ⓄⓄN / ⓄⓄ-NⓄ

A or **an** before a masculine noun:
He is (un) man.

Una / Un'

ⓄⓄN-ⒶⒽ / ⓄⓄN

A or **an** before a feminine noun:
She is (una) woman.

Some

Qualche

KWⒶⒽL-KⒺ

Some before masculine and feminine nouns.

USEFUL OPPOSITES

Near	Far
Vicino	Lontano
V**EE**-CH**EE**-N**O**	L**O**N-T**ah**-N**O**

Here	There
Qui	Là
KW**EE**	L**ah**

Left	Right
Sinistra	Destra
S**EE**-N**EE**S-TR**ah**	D**ĕ**S-TR**ah**

A little	A lot
Un poco	Molto
OON P**O**-K**O**	M**O**L-T**O**

More	Less
Di più	Meno
D**EE** P**EE**-**OO**	M**ĕ**-N**O**

Big	Small
Grande	Piccolo
GR**ah**N-D**ĕ**	P**EE**K-K**O**-L**O**

Open	Closed
Aperto	Chiuso
ah-PĔR-TO	KYOO-ZO

Cheap	Expensive
A buon mercato	Caro
ah BWON MĔR-Kah-TO	Kah-RO

Clean	Dirty
Pulito	Sporco
POO-LEE-TO	SPOR-KO

Good	Bad
Buono	Cattivo
BWO-NO	Kah-T-TEE-VO

Vacant	Occupied
Libero	Occupato
LEE-Bĕ-RO	O-KOO-Pah-TO

Right	Wrong
Giusto	Sbagliato
JOOS-TO	SBah-L-Yah-TO

WORDS OF ENDEARMENT

I love you.

Ti amo.

T︀EE ︀ah-MO

My love

Amore mio

ah-MO-Rĕ MEE-O

My life

Vita mia

VEE-Tah MEE-ah

My friend (to a male)

Amico mio

ah-MEE-KO MEE-O

My friend (to a female)

Amica mia

ah-MEE-Kah MEE-ah

Kiss me!

Baciami!

Bah-CHah-MEE

WORDS OF ANGER

What do you want?

Che cosa vuole?

Kĕ KŌ-Zah VWŌ-Lĕ

Leave me alone!

Mi lasci in pace!

MĒE Lah-SHĒE ĒN Pah-CHĕ

Go away!

Vada via!

Vah-Dah VĒE-ah

Stop bothering me!

Non mi stia a seccare!

NON MĒE STĒE-ah ah SĕK-Kah-Rĕ

Be quiet!

Silenzio!

SĒE-LĕN-TSĒE-O

That's enough!

Basta!

Bah'S-Tah

COMMON EXPRESSIONS

When you are at a loss for words but have the feeling you should say something, try one of these!

Who knows?

Chi lo sa?

K︎EE L︎O S︎ah

That's the truth!

E' la verità!

︎E L︎ah V︎E-R︎EE-T︎ah

Sure!

Sicuro!

S︎EE-K︎oo-R︎O

Wow!

Che sorpresa!

K︎E S︎OB-PR︎E-Z︎ah

What's happening?

Che cosa succede?

K︎E K︎O-Z︎ah S︎oo-CH︎E-D︎E

I think so.

Penso di sí.

P︎E-N-S︎O D︎EE S︎EE

Cheers!

Salute!

S@h-L@@-T@

Good luck!

Buona fortuna!

BW@-N@h F@B-T@@-N@h

With pleasure!

Con piacere!

K@N P@E-@h-CH@-B@

My goodness!

Per l'amor del cielo!

P@B L@h-M@B D@L CH@-L@

What a shame! / That's too bad!

Peccato!

P@K-K@h-T@

Well done! Bravo!

Bene! / Bravo!

B@-N@ / BB@h-V@

USEFUL COMMANDS

Stop!
Alt!
@LT

Go!
Forza!
FOR-TS@

Wait!
Aspetti!
@-SPĕT-TEE

Hurry!
Abbia fretta!
@B-BEE-Y@ FRĕT-T@

Slow down!
Rallenti!
R@L-LĕN-TEE

Come here!
Venga qui!
VĕN-G@ KWEE

Help!
Aiuto!
@-YOO-TO

EMERGENCIES

Fire!

Al fuoco!

@L FWO-KO

Emergency!

Emergenza!

ē-MēR-JēN-TS@

Call the police!

Chiamate la polizia!

KEE-@-M@-Tē L@ PO-LEE-TSEE-@

Call a doctor!

Chiamate un medico!

KEE-@-M@-Tē ooN Mē-DEE-KO

Call an ambulance!

Chiamate un' ambulanza!

KEE-@-M@-Tē ooN @M-Boo-L@N-TS@

I need help!

Ho bisogno d'aiuto!

O BEE-ZON-YO D@-Yoo-TO

ARRIVAL

Passing through customs should be easy since there are usually agents available who speak English. You may be asked how long you intend to stay and if you have anything to declare.

- Have your passport ready.
- Be sure all documents are up-to-date.
- While in a foreign country, it is wise to keep receipts for everything you buy.
- Be aware that many countries will charge a departure tax when you leave. Your travel agent should be able to find out if this affects you.
- If you have connecting flights, be sure to reconfirm them in advance.
- Make sure your luggage is clearly marked inside and out.
- Take valuables and medicines in carry-on bags.

SIGNS TO LOOK FOR:
DOGANA (Customs)
BAGAGLI (Baggage)

KEY WORDS

Baggage

Bagaglio

Bah-Gahĺ-YO

Customs

Dogana

DO-Gahí-Nah

Documents

Documenti

DO-Koo-MéN-TEE

Passport

Passaporto

PahS-Sah-POŔ-TO

Porter

Facchino

Fah-KEE-NO

Tax

Imposta

EEM-POŚ-Tah

USEFUL PHRASES

Here is my passport.

Ecco il mio passaporto.

Ĕ-KO ĔL MĒ-O Pah-S-Sah-PŌR-TO

I have nothing to declare.

Non ho nulla da dichiarare.

NON O NooL-Lah Dah
DĒ-KĒ-ah-Rah-Rĕ

I'm here on business.

Sono in viaggio d'affari.

SŌ-NO ĔN VĒ-ah-JO DahF-Fah-RĒ

I'm here on vacation.

Sono in vacanza.

SŌ-NO ĔN Vah-Kah'N-TSah

Is there a problem?

C'è un problema?

CHĕ ooN PRO-BLĕ-Mah

PHRASEMAKER

I'll be staying...

Resterò qui...

RⒺS-TⒺ´-RⓄ KWⒺⒺ...

▶ **one week**

una settimana

ⓄⓄ´-Nⓐⓗ SⒺT-TⒺⒺ-Mⓐⓗ´-Nⓐⓗ

▶ **two weeks**

due settimane

DⓄⓄ´-Ⓔ SⒺT-TⒺⒺ-Mⓐⓗ´-NⒺ

▶ **one month**

un mese

ⓄⓄN MⒺ´-SⒺ

▶ **two months**

due mesi

DⓄⓄ´-Ⓔ MⒺ´-SⒺⒺ

USEFUL PHRASES

I need a porter!

Ho bisogno di facchino!

Ⓞ　Bⓔⓔ-Z`Ⓞ`N-YⓄ　Dⓔⓔ　Fⓐⓗ-Kⓔⓔ-NⓄ

These are my bags.

Queste sono le mie valigia.

KWⓔ'S-Tⓔ　S`Ⓞ'`-NⓄ　Lⓔ
Mⓔⓔ'-ⓔ　Vⓐⓗ-Lⓔⓔ'-Jⓐⓗ

I'm missing a bag.

Mi manca una valigia.

Mⓔⓔ　Mⓐⓗ'N-Kⓐⓗ　ⓞⓞ'-Nⓐⓗ　Vⓐⓗ-Lⓔⓔ'-Jⓐⓗ

Take my bags to a taxi, please.

Per favore, porti le mie valigie al tassì.

Pⓔ'R　Fⓐⓗ-V`Ⓞ'`-Rⓔ　P`Ⓞ'`R-Tⓔⓔ　Lⓔ
Mⓔⓔ'-ⓔ　Vⓐⓗ-Lⓔⓔ'-Jⓔ　ⓐⓗL　TⓐⓗS-Sⓔⓔ'

Thank you. This is for you.

Grazie. Questo è per lei.

GRⓐⓗ'-TSⓔⓔ-ⓔ.
KWⓔ'S-TⓄ　ⓔ　Pⓔ'R　Lⓔ-ⓔⓔ

PHRASEMAKER

Where is...

Dov'è...

DO-Vế...

▶ **customs?**

dogana?

DO-Gằ-Nằ

▶ **baggage claim?**

il ritiro bagagli?

ẾL Rế-Tế-RO Bằ-Gằ-Lế

▶ **the money exchange?**

l'ufficio di cambio?

Lᴼᴼᴼᴼᴼᴼᴼᴼᴼᴼᴼᴼᴼᴼᴼᴼᴼᴼᴼᴼᴼᴼᴼᴼ

Lᴼᴼᴼ-Fế-CHO Dế Kằ'M-Bế-O

▶ **the taxi stand?**

il posteggio di taxi?

ẾL PO-STế-JO Dế Tằ S-Sế

▶ **the bus stop?**

la fermata dell'autobus?

Lằ Fế R-Mằ-Tằ Dế L ᴼᵂ-TO-BᴼᴼS

HOTEL SURVIVAL

A wide selection of accommodations, ranging from the most basic to the most extravagant, are available wherever you travel in Italy. When booking your room, find out what amenities are included for the price you pay.

- Make reservations well in advance and get written confirmation of your reservations before you leave home.

- Always have identification ready when checking in.

- Do not leave valuables, prescriptions, or cash in your room when you are not there!

- Electrical items like blow-dryers may need an adapter. Your hotel may be able to provide one, but to be safe, take one with you.

- Although a service charge is usually included on your bill, it is customary to tip maids, bellhops, and doormen.

KEY WORDS

Hotel

Hotel

Ⓞ-TⓔL

Bellman

Fattorino

FⓐT-TⓄ-RⒺⒺ-NⓄ

Maid

Cameriera

Kⓐ-Mⓔ-RⒺⒺ-ⓔ-Rⓐ

Message

Messaggio

MⓔS-Sⓐ-JⓄ

Reservation

Prenotazione

PRⓔ-NⓄ-Tⓐ-TSⒺⒺ-Ⓞ-Nⓔ

Room service

Servizio in camera

SⓔR-VⒺⒺ-TSⒺⒺ-Ⓞ ⒺⒺN Kⓐ-Mⓔ-Rⓐ

CHECKING IN

My name is...

Mi chiamo...

MEE KEE-ah-MO...

I have a reservation.

Ho una prenotazione.

O oo-Nah PRE-NO-Tah-TSEE-O-NE

Have you any vacancies?

Avete stanze libere?

ah-VE-TE STahN-TSE LEE-BE-RE

What is the charge per night?

Quanto costa per notte?

KWahN-TO KOS-Tah PER NOT-TE

Is there room service?

C'è il servizio in camera?

CHE EEL SER-VEE-TSEE-O EEN Kah-ME-Rah

PHRASEMAKER

I would like a room with...

Vorrei una stanza con…

VO-RĒ'-EE OO'-Nah STah'N-TSah KON…

▸ **a bath**

un bagno

OON Bah'N-YO

▸ **one bed**

un letto

OON LĒ'T-TO

▸ **two beds**

due letti

DOO'-Ē LĒ'T-TEE

▸ **a shower**

una doccia

OO'-Nah DŌ'-CHah

▸ **a view**

una vista

OO'-Nah VEE'S-Tah

USEFUL PHRASES

Where is the dining room?

Dov'è la sala da pranzo?

DO-Vě Lah Sah-Lah Dah PRah-N-TSO

Are meals included?

I pasti sono inclusi?

EE Pah-S-TEE SO-NO EN-KL-oo-ZEE

What time is breakfast?

A che ora è la colazione?

ah Kě O-Rah ě Lah

KO-Lah-TSEE-O-Ně

What time is lunch?

A che ora è il pranzo?

ah Kě O-Rah ě EEL PRah-N-TSO

What time is dinner?

A che ora è la cena?

ah Kě O-Rah ě Lah CHě-Nah

My room key, please.

La chiave, per favore.

Lⓐⓗ KⒺⒺ-ⓐⓗ'-Vⓔ PⓔⓇ Fⓐⓗ-VⓄ'-Ⓡⓔ

Are there any messages for me?

Ci sono dei messaggi per me?

CHⒺⒺ SⓄ'-NⓄ DⓔⒺⒺ Mⓔⓢ-Sⓐⓗ'-JⒺⒺ
PⓔⓇ Mⓔ

Please wake me at...

Per favore mi svegli alle...

PⓔⓇ Fⓐⓗ-VⓄ'-Ⓡⓔ MⒺⒺ
SVⓔ'L-YⒺⒺ ⓐⓗ'L-Lⓔ...

6:00	6:30
sei	sei e mezzo
Sⓔ'-ⒺⒺ	Sⓔ'-ⒺⒺ ⓔ Mⓔ'-TSⓄ

7:00	7:30
sette	sette e mezzo
Sⓔ'T-Tⓔ	Sⓔ'T-Tⓔ ⓔ Mⓔ'-TSⓄ

8:00	8:30
otto	otto e mezzo
ⓄT-TⓄ	ⓄT-TⓄ ⓔ Mⓔ'-TSⓄ

9:00	9:30
nove	nove e mezzo
NⓄ'-Vⓔ	NⓄ'-Vⓔ ⓔ Mⓔ'-TSⓄ

PHRASEMAKER

I need...

Ho bisogno...

Ⓞ BⒺⒺ-ZⓄ'N-YⓄ...

▸ **a babysitter**

di una babysitter

DⒺⒺ ⓄⓄ'-Nⓐⓗ Bⓔ-BⒺⒺ-SⒺⒺ'-TⓔR

▸ **a bellman**

di un fattorino

DⒺⒺ ⓄⓄN FⓐⓗT-TⓄ-RⒺⒺ'-NⓄ

▸ **more blankets**

di altre coperte

DⒺⒺ ⓐⓗ'L-TRⓔ KⓄ-PⓔR-Tⓔ

▸ **a hotel safe**

di una cassaforte

DⒺⒺ ⓄⓄ'-Nⓐⓗ Kⓐⓗ-Sⓐⓗ-FⓄ'R-Tⓔ

▸ **ice cubes**

di cubetti di ghiaccio

DⒺⒺ KⓄⓄ-BⓔT-TⒺⒺ DⒺⒺ GⒺⒺ-ⓐⓗ'-CHⓄ

▶ **an extra key**

di una chiave extra

DEE ꝏ-Nah KEE-ah-VE EKS-TRah

▶ **a maid**

di una cameriera

DEE ꝏ-Nah Kah-ME-REE-E-Rah

▶ **the manager**

del direttore

DEL DEE-RET-TO-RE

▶ **clean sheets**

di lenzuola pulite

DEE LEN-TSWO-Lah Pꝏ-LEE-TEE

▶ **soap**

di sapone

DEE Sah-PO-NE

▶ **toilet paper**

di carta igienica

DEE Kah-R-Tah EE-JE-NEE-Kah

▶ **more towels**

di altri asciugamani

DEE ahL-TREE ah-SHꝏ-Gah-Mah-NEE

PHRASEMAKER
(PROBLEMS)

There is no...

Manca...

M@N-K@...

▶ **electricity**

la corrente

L@ KO-R@N-T@

▶ **heat**

il riscaldamento

@L R@S-K@L-D@-M@N-1

▶ **hot water**

l'acqua calda

L@-KW@ K@L-D@

▶ **light**

la luce

L@ L@-CH@

▶ **toilet paper**

di carta igienica

D@ K@R-T@ @-J@-N@-K@

PHRASEMAKER
(SPECIAL NEEDS)

Do you have...

Avete...

ⓐ-Vⓔ́-Tⓔ...

▸ **an elevator?**

un ascensore?

ⓞⓞN ⓐ-SHⓔN-Sⓞ́-Bⓔ

▸ **a ramp?**

una rampa d'accesso?

ⓞⓞ́-Nⓐ Bⓐ́M-Pⓐ Dⓐ-CHⓔ́-Sⓞ

▸ **a wheelchair?**

una sedia a rotelle?

ⓞⓞ́-Nⓐ Sⓔ́D-Yⓐ ⓐ Bⓞ-Tⓔ́L-Lⓔ

▸ **facilities for the disabled?**

accomodamenti per gli handicappati?

ⓐ-Kⓞ-Mⓞ-Dⓐ-Mⓔ́N-TⒺ Pⓔ́B GLⒺ
ⓐN-DⒺ-Kⓐ́P-Pⓐ́-TⒺ

CHECKING OUT

I would like the bill, please.

Vorrei il conto, per favore.

VO-RĕÉ-EE EEL KOÍN-TO PF

Is this bill correct?

Questo conto è esatto?

KWĕS-TO KOÍN-TO ĕ ĕ-Zah́T-TO

Do you accept credit cards?

Accettate carte di credito?

ah-CHĕ-Tah́-Tĕ Kah́R-Tĕ DEE
KRĕ-DEE-TO

Could you have my luggage brought down?

Potrebbe far portare giù le mie valigie?

PO-TRĕ́-Bĕ Fah́R POR-Tah́-Rĕ
Joo Lĕ MEE-ĕ Vah-LĕÉ-Jĕ

Can you call a taxi for me?

Potrebbe chiamarmi un tassì?

PO-TRĕ́B-Bĕ KEE-ah-Mah́R-MEE
ooN Tah́S-SEÉ

I had a very good time!

Ho passato dei giorni bellissimi!

Ⓞ Pⓐ̲S-Sⓐ̲́-TⓄ Dⓔ̆ JⓄ́R-Nⓔ̲Ⓔ

Bⓔ̆L-Lⓔ̲Ⓔ́S-Sⓔ̲Ⓔ-Mⓔ̲Ⓔ

Thanks for everything.

Grazie di tutto.

GRⓐ̲́-TSⓔ̲Ⓔ Dⓔ̲Ⓔ Tⓞⓞ́T-TⓄ

I'll see you next time.

Arrivederci a presto.

ⓐ̲-Rⓔ̲Ⓔ-Vⓔ̆-Dⓔ̆́R-CHⓔ̲Ⓔ ⓐ̲ PRⓔ̆́S-TⓄ

Good-bye

Arrivederci

ⓐ̲-Rⓔ̲Ⓔ-Vⓔ̆-Dⓔ̆́R-CHⓔ̲Ⓔ

RESTAURANT SURVIVAL

Italy is famous for its cuisine. You are encouraged to enjoy the wide variety of regional specialties. Don't forget to try the many excellent Italian white wines and robust red wines!

- Breakfast, **la prima colazione**, is usually served at your hotel. Lunch, **il pranzo**, normally served from noon to 3 PM, and dinner, **la cena**, from 7 PM to 10 PM.

- Taste Italian cooking at the best-known **restaurantes** in the cities or try the many small **trattories** available. Many mouth-watering dishes await the adventurous traveler.

- **Pane e Coperto** indicates bread and cover charge. Most restaurants will have a cover charge and you will be charged even if you don't eat the bread!

- Some restaurants have a stand-up bar where you can order food and drinks with no cover charge.

- **Ristorante** offers fine dining and usually opens around 8:00 PM.

KEY WORDS

Breakfast

Colazione

KO-L@-TSEE-O-Nĕ

Lunch

Pranzo

PR@N-TSO

Dinner

Cena

CHĕ-N@

Waiter

Cameriere

K@-Mĕ-REE-ĕ-Rĕ

Waitress

Cameriera

K@-Mĕ-REE-ĕ-R@

Restaurant

Ristorante

REES-TO-R@N-Tĕ

USEFUL PHRASES

A table for...

Un tavolo per...

ⓄN Tⓐⓗ-Vⓞ-Lⓞ Pⓔⓡ...

2	4	6
due	quattro	sei
Dⓞⓞ-ⓔ	KWⓐⓗT-TⓡⓄ	S④

The menu, please.

Il menù, per favore.

ⒺⒺL Mⓔ-Nⓞⓞ PF

Separate checks, please.

Conti separati, per favore.

KⓄN-TⒺⒺ Sⓔ-Pⓐⓗ-Rⓐⓗ-TⒺⒺ PF

We are in a hurry.

Abbiamo fretta.

ⓐⓗB-BⒺⒺ-ⓐⓗ-MⓄ FRⓔT-Tⓐⓗ

What do you recommend?

Che cosa consiglia?

Kⓔ KⓄ-Zⓐⓗ KⓄN-SⒺⒺL-Yⓐⓗ

Please bring me...

Per favore, mi porti...

PⓔR Fⓐ-VⓄ-Rⓔ Mⓔⓔ PⓄR-Tⓔⓔ

Please bring us...

Per favore ci porti...

PⓔR Fⓐ-VⓄ-Rⓔ CHⓔⓔ PⓄR-Tⓔⓔ

I'm hungry.

Ho fame.

Ⓞ Fⓐ-Mⓔ

I'm thirsty.

Ho sete.

Ⓞ Sⓔ-Tⓔ

Is service included?

Il servizio e incluso?

ⓔⓔL SⓔR-Vⓔⓔ-TSⓔⓔ-Ⓞ ⓔ ⓔⓔN-KLⓄⓄ-ZⓄ

I would like the bill, please.

Vorrei il conto, per favore.

VⓄ-Rⓔ-ⓔⓔ ⓔⓔL
KⓄN-TⓄ PF

PHRASEMAKER

Ordering beverages is easy and a great way to practice your Italian! In many foreign countries you will have to request ice with your drinks.

Please bring me...

Per favore, mi porti...

PĔR F@H-VŌ-RĔ MĒ PŌR-TĒĒ...

▸ **coffee**

del caffè

DĔL K@H-FĒ

▸ **tea**

del tè

DĔL TĒ

▸ **with cream**

con panna

KON P@HN-N@H

▸ **with sugar**

con zucchero

TSOO-KĒ-RO

▸ **with lemon**

con limone

KON LĒĒ-MŌ-NĒ

▸ **with ice**

con ghiaccio

KON GĒĒ-@H-CHO

Soft drinks

Bibite

BEE-BEE-Tĕ

Milk

Latte

LahT-Tĕ

Hot chocolate

Cioccolata

CHOK-KO-Lah-Tah

Juice

Succo

TSooK-KO

Orange juice

Succo d'arancia

TSoo-KO DEE ah-Rah'N-CHah

Ice water

Acqua con ghiaccio

ah-KWah KON GEE-ah-CHO

Mineral water

Acqua minerale

ah-KWah MEE-Nĕ-Rah-Lĕ

AT THE BAR

Bartender

Barista

B@h-R@S-T@h

The wine list, please.

La lista dei vini, per favore.

L@h L@S-T@h D@@ V@-N@ PF

Cocktail

Cocktail

K@K-T@L

On the rocks

Con ghiaccio

K@N G@-@-CH@

Straight

Senza ghiaccio

S@N-TS@h G@-@-CH@

With lemon

Con limone

K@N L@-M@-N@

PHRASEMAKER

I would like a glass of...

Vorrei un bicchiere di...

VO-Rê-EE oON BEEK-Yê-Rê...

▸ **champagne**

champagne

SHaM-PaN-Yah

▸ **beer**

birra

BEER-Rah

▸ **wine**

vino

VEE-NO

▸ **red wine**

vino rosso

VEE-NO ROS-SO

▸ **white wine**

vino bianco

VEE-NO BEE-aN-KO

Complement your meal with a variety of choices of sparkling wines, roses, liqueurs, and the grappas!

ORDERING BREAKFAST

In Italy, breakfast is usually small, consisting of a croissant or warm bread with butter and jam accompanied by café au lait, hot tea, or hot chocolate.

Bread	**Toast**
Pane	Pane tostato
Pⓐⱨ-Nⓔ	Pⓐⱨ-Nⓔ TⓄS-Tⓐⱨ-TⓄ

with butter

con burro

KⓄN   Bⓞⱺ-RⓄ

with jam

con marmellata

KⓄN   MⓐⱨR-Mⓔ̃L-Lⓐⱨ-Dⓐⱨ

Cereal

Cereali

CHⒶ-RⒶ-ⓐⱨ-Lⓔⓔ

PHRASEMAKER

I would like...

Vorrei...

VO-Rĕ-EE...

▶ **two eggs...**

due uova...

DOO-ĕ WO-Vah

▶ **scrambled**

strapazzate

STRah-Pah-TSah-Tĕ

▶ **fried**

fritte

FREET-Tĕ

▶ **with bacon**

con pancetta

KON Pah-N-CHĕ-Tah

▶ **with ham**

con prosciutto

KON PRO-SHOOT-TO

▶ **with potatoes**

con patate

KON Pah-Tah-Tĕ

LUNCH AND DINNER

Although you are encouraged to sample great Italian cuisine, it is important to be able to order foods you are familiar with. This section will provide words and phrases to help you.

I would like...

Vorrei....

VO'-Rĕ-EE...

We would like...

Vorremmo...

VO-Rĕ̃M-MO...

Please bring us...

Per favore ci porti...

PĕR Fah-VO-Rĕ CHEE PO'R-TEE...

The lady would like...

La signora vorrebbe...

Lah SEEN-YO'-Rah VO-Rĕ̃B-Bĕ...

The gentleman would like...

Il signore vorrebbe...

EEL SEEN-YO'-Rĕ VO-Rĕ̃B-Bĕ...

STARTERS

Appetizers

Antipasti

@N-T€€-P@'S-T€

Bread and butter

Pane e burro

P@'-N€ € B@'-R@

Cheese

Formaggio

F@R-M@'-J@

Fruit

Frutta

FR@'T-T@

Salad

Insalata

€N-S@-L@'-T@

Soup

Zuppa

TS@'P-P@

MEATS

Bacon
Pancetta
P@N-CH@T-T@

Beef
Manzo
M@N-TS@

Beef steak
Bistecca
B@S-T@K-K@

Ham
Prosciutto
PR@-SH@T-T@

Lamb
Agnello
@N-Y@L-L@

Pork
Maiale
M@-Y@-L@

Veal
Vitello
V@-T@L-L@

POULTRY

Roasted chicken

Pollo al forno

PŎL-LŎ aL FŎR-NŎ

Broiled chicken

Pollo alla griglia

PŎL-LŎ aL-La GRĒL-Ya

Fried chicken

Pollo fritto

PŎL-LŎ FRĒT-TŎ

Duck

Anitra

a-NĒ-TRa

Goose

Oca

Ŏ-Ka

Turkey

Tacchino

Ta-KĒ-NŎ

SEAFOOD

Fish
Pesce
PĒ-SHĒ

Lobster
Aragosta
ah-Rah-GŌS-Tah

Oysters
Ostriche
ŌS-TRĒE-KĒ

Salmon
Salmone
Sah-L-MŌ-NĒ

Shrimp
Gamberetti
Gah-M-BĒ-RĒT-TEE

Trout
Trota
TRŌ-Tah

Tuna
Tonno
TŌN-NŌ

OTHER ENTREES

Sandwich
Panino
P@-NEE-N@

Hot dog
Hot dog
@T D@G

Hamburger
Hamburger
@M-B@-G@R

French fries
Patatine fritte
P@-T@-TEE-N@ FREET-T@

Pasta
Pasta
P@S-T@

Pizza
Pizza
PEET-S@

VEGETABLES

Carrots

Carote

K@h-R@'-T@

Corn

Granturco

GR@N-T@R-K@

Mushrooms

Funghi

F@N-G@

Onions

Cipolle

CH@-P@L-L@

Potatoes

Patate

P@-T@'-T@

Rice

Riso

R@'-Z@

Tomato

Pomodoro

P@-M@-D@'-R@

FRUITS

Apple

Mela

MĔ-L@h

Banana

Banana

B@h-N@h-N@h

Grapes

Uva

oo-V@h

Lemon

Limone

LEE-MO-NĔ

Orange

Arancia

@h-R@hN-CH@h

Strawberry

Fragola

FR@h-GO-L@h

Watermelon

Anguria

@hN-Goo-REE-@h

DESSERTS

Desserts
Dolci
DŌL-CHEE

Apple pie
Crostata di mela
KROS-Tah-Tah DEE MĚ-Lah

Cherry pie
Crostata di ciliegia
KROS-Tah-Tah DEE CHEL-Yě-Jě

Pastries
Pasticcini
PahS-TEE-CHEE-NEE

Candy
Caramella
Kah-Rah-MĚL-Lah

Order a refreshing strawberry or lemon sorbet as the
perfect end to your lovely Italian meal!

Ice cream

Gelato

JÉ-Lah-TO

Ice-cream cone

Cono di gelato

KO-NO DEE JÉ-Lah-TO

Chocolate

Cioccolata

CHOK-KO-Lah-Tah

Strawberry

Fragola

FRah-GO-Lah

Vanilla

Vaniglia

Vah-NEEL-Yah

CONDIMENTS

Butter
Burro
Bₓ-Rₓ

Ketchup
Ketchup
Kĕ-CHₓP

Mayonnaise
Maionese
M@-YO-Nĕ-Sĕ

Mustard
Senape
Sĕ-N@-Pĕ

Salt	**Pepper**
Sale	Pepe
S@-Lĕ	Pĕ-Pĕ

Sugar
Zucchero
TSₓ-Kĕ-Rₓ

Vinegar and oil
Aceto e olio
@-CHĕ-TO   ĕ   OL-YO

SETTINGS

A cup
Una tazza
OO'-Nah Tah'-TSah

A glass
Un bicchiere
OON BEEK-Yeh'-Reh

A spoon
Un cucchiaio
OON KOOK-Yah'-YO

A fork
Una forchetta
OO'-Nah FOR-Keh'T-Tah

A knife
Un coltello
OON KOL-Teh'L-LO

A plate
Un piatto
OON PEE-ah'T-TO

A napkin
Un tovagliolo
OON TO-Vah'L-YO'-LO

HOW DO YOU WANT IT COOKED?

Baked

Al forno

@L FOŘ-NO

Broiled

Al graticola

@L GŘah-TEE-KO-Lah

Steamed

Al vapore

@L Vah-PO-Ře

Fried

Fritte

FŘEET-Te

Rare

Al sangue

@L Sah'N-GWe

Medium

Cotta normale

KOT-Tah NOŘ-Mah-Le

Well done

Ben cotta

Be'N KOT-Tah

PROBLEMS

I didn't order this.

Non ho ordinato questo.

NON O OR-DEE-Nah-TO KWeS-TO

Is the bill correct?

Il conto è esatto?

EL KON-TO e e-Zah'T-TO

Please bring me...

Per favore, mi porti...

PeR Fah-VO-Re Me POR-Te

GETTING AROUND

Getting around in a foreign country can be an adventure in itself! Taxi (**Tassì**) and bus drivers do not always speak English, so it is essential to be able to give simple directions. The words and phrases in this chapter will help you get where you're going.

- The best way to get a taxi is at a taxi stand. Taxis have meters that are preset with different amounts depending on the time of day.

- Trains are used frequently by visitors to Europe. They are efficient and provide connections between large cities and towns throughout the country. Arrive early to allow time for ticket purchasing and checking in, and remember, trains leave on time!

- **Stazione della Metropolitana** or subway in Italy offers an easy way to get around. A red **"M"** usually indicates a subway stop.

- Check with your travel agent about special rail passes which allow unlimited travel within a set period of time.

KEY WORDS

Airport

Aeroporto

@ⓗ-ⓔ-Ⓡⓞ-Pⓞ́B-Tⓞ

Bus Station / Bus Stop

Stazione dell'autobus

Fermata dell'autobus

ST@ⓗ-TSⒺ-Ⓞ́-Nⓔ̈ DⓔL Ⓞw-Tⓞ-BⓞⓞS

FⓔB-M@ⓗ-T@ⓗ DⓔL Ⓞw-Tⓞ-BⓞⓞS

Car Rental Agency

Agenzia di autonoleggio

@ⓗ-Jⓔ̈N-TSⒺ-Y@ⓗ DⒺ Ⓞw-Tⓞ-Nⓞ-Lⓔ̈-CHⓞ

Subway Station

Stazione della metropolitana

ST@ⓗ-TSⒺ-Ⓞ́-Nⓔ̈ Dⓔ̈-L@ⓗ

Mⓔ̈-TBⓞ-Pⓞ-LⒺ-T@ⓗ-N@ⓗ

Taxi Stand

Posteggio di tassì

Pⓞ-STⓔ̈-Jⓞ DⒺ T@ⓗS-Sⓔ̈

Train Station

Stazione ferroviaria

ST@ⓗ-TSⒺ-Ⓞ́-Nⓔ̈ Fⓔ̈-Bⓞ-VⒺ-@ⓗ-BⒺ-@ⓗ

AIR TRAVEL

Arrivals
Arrivi
ah-BEE-VEE

Departures
Partenza
PahR-TEN-TSah

Flight number
Numero di volo
Noo-MEH-Ro DEE VO-Lo

Airline
Compagnia aerea
KOM-Pah-NEE-ah   ah-EH-REH-ah

Gate
Cancello
KahN-CHEL-Lo

Information
Informazione
EEN-FOR-Mah-TSEE-O-NEH

Ticket (airline)
Biglietto aereo
BEEL-YET-To   ah-EH-REH-O

Reservations
Prenotazioni
PREH-No-Tah-TSEE-O-NEE

PHRASEMAKER

I would like a seat...

Vorrei un posto...

VO-RĕĕE-ĕĕ ooN POS-TO...

▸ **in first class**

in prima classe

ĔĔN PRĔĔ-Mah KLahS-Sĕ

▸ **in the no-smoking section**

tra i non fumatori

TRah ĔĔ NON Foo-Mah-TO-RĔĔ

▸ **next to the window**

accanto al finestrino

ahK-Kah-N-TO ahL FĔĔ-NĕS-TRĔĔ-NO

▸ **on the aisle**

vicino al corridoio

VĔĔ-CHĔĔ-NO ahL KO-RĔĔ-DO-ĔĔ-O

▸ **near the exit**

vicino all'uscita

VĔĔ-CHĔĔ-NO ahL oo-SHĔĔ-Tah

BY BUS

Bus

Autobus

ow-TO-BOOS

Where is the bus stop?

Dov'è la fermata dell'autobus?

DO-Vě Lah FěR-Mah-Tah
DěL ow-TO-BOOS

Do you go to...?

Va a...?

Vah ah...

What is the fare?

Quanto costa il biglietto?

KWahN-TO KOS-Tah ěL BEEL-Yě-TO

Do I need exact change?

Bisogno del cambiamento esatto?

BEE-ZON-YO DěL
KahM-BEE-ah-MěN-TO ě-ZahT-TO

How often do the buses run?

Ogni quanti minuti corre l'autobus?

ON-YEE KWahN-TEE MEE-Noo-TEE
KOB-ě Low-TO-BOOS

PHRASEMAKER

Please tell me...

Per favore mi dica...

PĔR Fᵃʰ-VŌ-Rĕ MĒ DĒĒ-Kᵃʰ...

▸ **which bus goes to...**

quale autobus va a...

KWᵃʰ-Lĕ ⓞʷ-TO-BⓞⓞS Vᵃʰ ⓐʰ...

▸ **what time the bus leaves**

a che ora parte l'autobus

ⓐʰ KⒶ Ō-Rᵃʰ PᵃʰʳR-TⒶ
Lⓞʷ-TⓞⒷⓞⓞS

▸ **where the bus stop is**

dov'è la fermata dell'autobus

DⓄ-Vĕ Lᵃʰ FĔR-Mᵃʰ-Tᵃʰ
DĕL ⓞʷ-TⓄ-BⓞⓞS

▸ **when to get off**

quando devo scendere

KWᵃʰN-DⓄ DⒶ-VⓄ SHⒶN-DⒶ-Rᵃ

BY CAR

Fill it up.

Faccia il pieno.

F@-CH@ @L P@-@-N@

Can you help me?

Può aiutarmi?

PW@ @-Y@-T@B-M@

My car won't start.

La mia auto non funziona.

L@ M@-@ @-T@ N@N
F@N-TS@-@N-@

Can you fix it?

Può aggiustarla?

PW@ @-J@S-T@B-L@

What will it cost me?

Quanto mi costerà?

KW@N-T@ M@ K@S-T@-B@

How long will it take?

Quanto tempo ci sarà?

KW@N-T@ T@M-P@ CH@ S@-B@

PHRASEMAKER

Please check...

Per piacere...Per favore

PⓔR PⒺⒺ-ⓐ-CHⓔ-Rⓔ... PF

▶ **the battery**

la batteria

Lⓐ Bⓐ T-Tⓔ-RⒺⒺ-ⓐ

▶ **the brakes**

i freni

ⒺⒺ FRⓔ-Nⓔ

▶ **the oil**

l'olio

LⓄ-LⒺⒺ-Ⓞ

▶ **the tires**

le gomme

Lⓔ GⓄM-Mⓔ

▶ **the water**

l'acqua

Lⓐ-KWⓐ

SUBWAYS AND TRAINS

Where is the subway station?
Dov'è la stazione della metropolitana?

DO-Vḛ́ Lᵃʰ STᵃʰ-TSᴇᴇ-Ó-Nḛ
DḚ́L-Lᵃʰ Mḛ-TRO-PO-Lᴇᴇ-Tᵃʰ́-Nᵃʰ

Where is the train station?
Dov'è la stazione ferroviaria?

DO-Vḛ́ Lᵃʰ STᵃʰ-TSᴇᴇ-Ó-Nḛ
Fḛ-RO-Vᴇᴇ-ᵃʰ́-Rᴇᴇ-ᵃʰ

A one-way ticket, please.
Un biglietto di sola andanta, per piacere.

ᴏᴏN BᴇᴇL-Yḛ́T-TO Dᴇᴇ SO-Lᵃʰ
ᵃʰN-Dᵃʰ́N-Tᵃʰ   PPC

A round trip ticket
Un biglietto d'andata e ritorno

ᴏᴏN BᴇᴇL-Yḛ́-TO DᵃʰN-Dᵃʰ́-Tᵃʰ ḛ
Rᴇᴇ-TÓR-NO

First class
Prima classe

PRᴇᴇ́-Mᵃʰ KLᵃʰ́S-Sḛ

Second class
Seconda classe

Sḛ́-KÓN-Dᵃʰ KLᵃʰ́S-Sḛ

Which train do I take to go to...?

Quale treno devo prendere per andare a...?

KW@-L@ TR@-N© D@-V©
PR@N-D@-R@ P@R @N-D@-R@ @...

What is the fare?

Quanto costa il biglietto?

KW@N-T© K©S-T@ @L
B@L-Y@T-T©

Is this seat taken?

Questo posto è occupato?

KW@S-T© P©S-T© @
©-K@-P@-T©

Do I have to change trains?

Devo cambiar dei treni?

D@-V© K@M-B@-@R D@@ TR@-N@

Does this train stop at...?

Questo treno si ferma a...?

KW@S-T© TR@-N© S@ F@R-M@ @...

Where are we?

Dove siamo?

D©-V@ S@-@-M©

TAXI

Can you call a taxi for me?

Potrebbe chiamarmi un tassì?

PⓄ-TⓇⒺ̃B-BⒺ̃ KⒺⒺ-ⓐ-Mⓐ̃R-MⒺⒺ
ⓄⓄN Tⓐ̃S-SⒺⒺ

Are you available?

È libero?

Ⓔ̃ LⒺⒺ́-BⒺ̃-ⓇⓄ

I want to go to...

Vorrei andare a...

VⓄ-ⓇⒺ̃́-ⒺⒺ ⓐN-Dⓐ́-ⓇⒺ̃ ⓐ...

Stop here, please.

Si fermi qui, per favore.

SⒺⒺ FⒺ̃R-MⒺⒺ KWⒺⒺ PF

Please wait for me.

Mi aspetti, per favore.

MⒺⒺ ⓐ-SPⒺ̃́T-TⒺⒺ PF

How much do I owe?

Quanto le devo?

KWⓐ́N-TⓄ LⒺ̃ DⒺ̃́-VⓄ

PHRASEMAKER

I would like to go...

Vorrei andare...

VO-RĕE-EE ahN-Dah-Rĕ...

▶ **to this address**

a questo indirizzo

ah KWĕS-TO EEN-DEE-RĔET-TSO

▶ **to the airport**

all'aeroporto

ahL ah-ĕ-RO-POR-TO

▶ **to the bank**

all banca.

ahL BahN-Kah

▶ **to the hotel**

all'hotel

ahL O-TĕL

▶ **to the hospital**

all'ospedale

ahL OS-Pĕ-Dah-Lĕ

▶ **to the subway station**

alla stazione della metropolitana

ah-Lah STah-TSEE-O-Nĕ DĕL-Lah

Mĕ-TRO-PO-LEE-Tah-Nah

SHOPPING

Whether you plan a major shopping spree or just need to purchase some basic necessities, the following information is useful.

- Shops are usually open between 9 AM and 7 PM, closing two or three hours in the afternoon.

- I.V.A. (sales tax) rebate is available to tourists within 90 days of purchase. However, there is a minimum amount that must be spent and it must be in the same store in the same day.

- Always keep receipts for everything you buy! Your receipt must be stamped by Customs and mailed back to the vendor in order to qualify for a rebate.

SIGNS TO LOOK FOR:

FIORAIO (Florist)

FARMACIA (Pharmacy)

SUPERMERCATO (Supermarket)

GIOIELLERIA (Jewelry Store)

TABACCHERIA (Corner Store, stamps, newspaper, tickets, candy)

GELATERIA (Ice-cream store)

PANETTERIA (Bakery - Bread)

KEY WORDS

Credit card

Carta di credito

KⓐR-Tⓐ DⒺ KRⓔ-DⒺ-Tⓞ

Money

Denaro

DⓔN-Nⓐ-Rⓞ

Receipt

Ricevuta

RⒺ-CHⓔ-Vⓞⓞ-Tⓐ

Sale

Vendita

VⓔN-DⒺ-Tⓐ

Store

Negozio

Nⓔ-Gⓞ-TSⒺ-ⓞ

Traveler's checks

Traveler's check

TRⓐ-Vⓔ-LⓔRS CHⓔK

USEFUL PHRASES

Do you sell...?

Vende...?

VĚN-DĚ...

Do you have...?

Avete...?

ah-VĚ-TĚ...

I want to buy...

Vorrei comprare...

VO-RĚ-EE KOM-PRah-RĚ...

How much?

Quanto costa?

KWahN-TO KOS-Tah

When are the shops open?

Quando sono aperti i negozi?

KWahN-DO SO-NO ah-PĚR-TEE EE

NĚ-GOT-SEE

No, thank you.

No, grazie.

NO GRah-TSEE-Ě

I´m just looking.

Sto solo guardando.

STO SO-LO GWahR-DahN-DO

It's very expensive.

E'molto costoso.

ē MOL-TO KOS-TO-ZO

Could you give me a discount?

Potrebbe farmi uno sconto?

PO-TRēB-Bē FahR-MEE oo-NO
SKON-TO

I'll take it!

Lo prendo!

LO PRēN-DO

I'd like a receipt, please.

Vorrei la ricevuta, per favore.

VO-Rē-EE Lah REE-CHē-Voo-Tah PF

I want to return this.

Vorrei restituire questo.

VO-Rē-EE RēS-TEE-Too-EE-Rē
KWēS-TO

It doesn't fit.

Non è della mia misura.

NON ē DēL-Lah MEE-ah MEE-Soo-Rah

PHRASEMAKER

I'm looking for...

Sto cercando...

STⓄ CHⒺR-KⒶ'N-DⓄ...

▶ **a bakery**

una panetteria

ⓄⓄ'-Nⓐ Pⓐ-NⒺT-TⒺ-RⒺⒺ'-ⓐ

▶ **a bank**

una banca

ⓄⓄ'-Nⓐ Bⓐ'N-Kⓐ

▶ **a barber shop**

un barbiere

ⓄⓄ'-Nⓐ Bⓐ-BⒺⒺ'-Ⓔ'-RⒺ

▶ **a camera shop**

un negozio di macchine fotografiche

ⓄⓄN NⒺ'-GⓄ'-TSⒺⒺ-Ⓞ DⒺⒺ

Mⓐ'-KⒺⒺ-NⒺ FⓄ-TⓄ-GRⓐ'-FⒺⒺ-KⒺ

▶ **a hair salon**

un parrucchiere

ⓄⓄN Pⓐ-RⓄⓄK-KⒺⒺ-Ⓔ'-RⒺ

▶ **a pharmacy**

una farmacia

ⓄⓄ'-Nⓐ Fⓐ-Mⓐ-CHⒺⒺ'-ⓐ

PHRASEMAKER

Do you sell...

Vende...

VＥ̈N-DＥ̈...

▶ **aspirin?**

aspirina?

ＡｈS-PＥＥ-RＥＥ́-Nａｈ

▶ **cigarettes?**

sigarette?

SＥＥ-Gａｈ-RＥ̈́T-TＥ̈

▶ **deodorant?**

deodorante?

DＥ̈-Ｏ-DＯ-Rａｈ́N-TＥ̈

▶ **dresses?**

abiti da donna?

Ａｈ́-BＥＥ-TＥＥ   Dａｈ   DＯ́N-Nａｈ

▶ **film?**

rullini fotografici?

RＯＯL-LＥＥ́-NＥＥ   FＯ-TＯ-GRａｈ-FＥＥ́-CHＥＥ

▸ **pantyhose?**

collant?

KŌL-LⓐNT

▸ **perfume?**

profumo?

PRŌ-Fⓞⓞ-MŌ

▸ **razor blades?**

lamette?

Lⓐ-MⒺ́T-TⒺ

▸ **shampoo?**

shampoo?

SHⓐM-PŌ

▸ **shaving cream?**

crema da barba?

KRⒺ́-Mⓐ　Dⓐ　Bⓐ́R-Bⓐ

▸ **shirts?**

camicie?

Kⓐ-MⒺⒺ́-CHⒺ

▸ **soap?**

di sapone?

DⒺⒺ　Sⓐ-PṒ-NⒺ

▶ **sunglasses?**

occhiali da sole?

OK-KEE-ah'-LEE Dah SO'-Lĕ

▶ **sunscreen?**

crema antisolare?

KRĕ'-Mah ahN-TEE-SO-Lah'-Rĕ

▶ **toothbrushes?**

spazzolino da denti?

SPah T-TSO-LEE'-NO DA DĕN-TEE

▶ **toothpaste?**

dentifricio?

DĕN-TEE-FRĕ'-CHO

▶ **water? (bottled)**

bottiglie d'acqua?

BOT-TEE'-LYEE-ĕ Dah'-KWah

▶ **water? (mineral)**

acqua minerale?

ah'-KWah MEE-Nĕ-Rah'-Lĕ

ESSENTIAL SERVICES

THE BANK

As a traveler in a foreign country your primary contact with banks will be to exchange money. Keep in mind that many banks close in the afternoon and on Saturday and Sunday.

- The Italian national currency is the euro. Bank notes are in denominations of Euro 500, 200, 100, 50, 20, 10, and 5. Coins are in denominations of 2 and 1 euro, and 50, 20, 10, 5, 2, and 1 euro cents.

- Change enough funds before leaving home to pay for tips, food, and transportation to your final destination.

- Generally, you will receive a better rate of exchange at a bank, but rates can change from bank to bank. Exchange offices are found at airports, some train stations, and tourist sites.

- Current exchange rates are posted in banks and published daily in city newspapers.

- ATM machines are readily available. In Italy, they are known as **Bancomat**. Traveler's checks and credit cards are accepted in most major tourist cities.

KEY WORDS

Bank

Banca

BⓐN-Kⓐ

Exchange office

Ufficio di cambio

ⓄⓄ-FⒺⒺ-CHⓄ DⒺⒺ KⓐM-BⒺⒺ-Ⓞ

Money

Denaro

DⒺ-Nⓐ-RⓄ

Money order

Mandato di pagamento

MⓐN-Dⓐ-TⓄ DⒺⒺ Pⓐ-Gⓐ-MⒺN-TⓄ

Traveler's checks

Traveler's checks

TRⓐ-VⒺ-LⒺRS CHⒺKS

USEFUL PHRASES

Where is the bank?

Dov'è la banca?

DO-Vё Lah BahN-Kah

What time does the bank open?

A che ora apre la banca?

ah Kё O-Rah ah-PRё Lah
BahN-Kah

Where is the exchange office?

Dov'è l'ufficio di cambio?

DO-Vё Loo-Fёё-CHO Dёё
KahM-Bёё-O

What time does the exchange office open?

A che ora apre l'ufficio di cambio?

ah Kё O-Rah ah-PRё
Loo-Fёё-CHO Dёё KahM-Bёё-O

Can I change dollars here?

Posso cambiare i dollari qui?

POS-SO KahM-Bёё-ah-Rё ёё
DOL-Lah-Rёё KWёё

Can you change this?

Può cambiarmi questo?

PWO KahM-BEE-ahR-MEE KWēS-TO

What is the exchange rate?

Qual'è il cambio?

KWah-Lē EEL KahM-BEE-O

I would like large bills.

Vorrei banconote di grosso taglio.

VO-Rē-EE BahN-KO-NO-Tē DEE
GROS-SO TahL-YO

I would like small bills.

Vorrei banconote di grosso taglio.

VO-Rē-EE BahN-KO-NO-Tē DEE

I need change. (coins)

Ho bisogno moneta riccola.

O BEE-ZON-YO MO-Nē-Tē
REE-KO-Lah

Do you have an ATM?

Avete un bancomat?

ah-Vē-Tē OON BahN-KO-MahT

POST OFFICE

POSTE E TELECOMUNI-CAZIONI or PT identify the post office. Stamps can be purchased at a **tabaccheria** as well as in certain cafés and post offices.

KEY WORDS

Airmail

Via aerea

VEE-ah ah-ě-REE-ah

Letter

Lettera

LěT-T Ⓐ-Rah

Post office

Ufficio postale

ⓞⓞF-FEE-CHⓞ PⓞS-Tah-LⒶ

Postcard

Cartolina postale

Kah R-TⓄ-LEE-Nah PⓄS-Tah-LⒶ

Stamps

Francobolli

FRah N-KⓄ-BⓄL-LEE

USEFUL PHRASES

Where is the post office?

Dov'è l'ufficio postale?

DO-Vĕ́ LOO-FḖ-CHO POS-Tah́-Lĕ

What time does the post office open?

A che ora apre l'ufficio postale?

ah Kĕ́ O-Rah ah-PRĕ
LOO-FḖ-CHO POS-Tah́-Lĕ

I need stamps.

Ho bisogno di francobolli.

O BĒ-ZÓN-YO DĒ
FRah-N-KO-BÓL-LĒ

I need an envelope.

Ho bisogno d'una busta.

O BĒ-ZÓN-YO DOO-Nah BOOS-Tah

I need a pen.

Ho bisogno d'una penna.

O BĒ-ZÓN-YO DOO-Nah PĔ́N-Nah

TELEPHONE

Placing phone calls in a foreign country can be a test of will and stamina! Besides the obvious language barriers, service can vary greatly from one town to the next.

- In Italy, phone calls can be made from the post office, especially long-distance calls.

- It is a good idea to purchase a phone card on arrival in Italy at the airport or train station. Newsstands and tobacco shops also sell phone cards.

- **Tabaccheria** is the local corner store where you can purchase phone cards, newspapers, stamps, tickets, candy, etc.

- Long-distance calls can be dialed on public telephones. Most use phone cards. When you use a phone card, you will reach an operator that speaks the language of the destination call.

KEY WORDS

Information

Informazione

ⒺN-FOR-Mah-TSⒺⒺ-O'-Nⓔ

Long distance

Interurbano

ⒺN-Tⓔ-Roor-Bah-NO

Operator

Signorina / Centralino

SⒺⒺN-YO-RⒺⒺ-Nah / CHⓔN-TRah-LⒺⒺ-NO

Phone book

Elenco telefonica

ⓔ-Lⓔ'N-KO Tⓔ-Lⓔ-FO'-NⒺⒺ-Kah

Public telephone

Telefono pubblico

Tⓔ-Lⓔ'-FO-NO Poo'B-BLⒺⒺ-KO

Telephone

Telefono

Tⓔ-Lⓔ'-FO-NO

USEFUL PHRASES

May I use your telephone?

Posso usare il suo telefono?

PÓS-SO oo-Zah-Rĕ ĔL Sŏo-O Tĕ-Lĕ-FO-NO

I don't speak Italian.

Non parlo italiano.

NON Pah-R-LO ĔE-Tah-LĔE-ah-NO

I would like to make a call long distance.

Vorrei fare una telefonata interurbana.

VO-Rĕ-ĔE Fah-Rĕ oo-Nah Tā-Lā-FO-Nah-Tah ĔN-Tĕ-RooR-Bah-Nah

I would like to make a call to the United States.

Vorrei fare una telefonata agli stati uniti.

VO-Rĕ-ĔE Fah-Rĕ oo-Nah Tā-Lā-FO-Nah-Tah ah-LYĔE STah-TĔE oo-NĔE-TĔE

I want to call this number...

Vorrei chiamare questo numero...

VO-Rĕ́-EE KEE-ah-Mah-Rĕ KWĕ́S-TO
NOO-Mĕ́-RO...

1 uno OO-NO	**2** due DOO-ĕ	**3** tre TRĕ́
4 quattro KWah́-TRO	**5** cinque CHĔ́N-KWĕ	**6** sei Sĕ́EE
7 sette Sĕ́T-Tĕ	**8** otto Ó T-TO	**9** nove NÓ́-Vĕ
✳	**0** zero Zĕ́-RO	**#**

SIGHTSEEING AND ENTERTAINMENT

In most towns in Italy you will find tourist information offices. Here you can usually obtain brochures, maps, historical information, bus and train schedules.

There are many ways to discover Italy from concerts, plays, and festivals to beautiful open-air squares and streets. Visit beautiful churches, palaces, monuments, castles, and museums or just relax and enjoy a cappuccino or glass of wine!

ITALIAN CITIES

Roma (Rome)
RŌ-Mah

Napoli (Naples)
Nah-PŌ-LEE

Milano (Milan)
MEE-Lah-NŌ

Pisa (Pisa)
PEE-Zah

Venezia (Venice)
Vĕ-NĕT-SEE-ah

Firenze (Florence)
FEE-RĕN-TSA

KEY WORDS

Admission

Entrata

ĕN-TRah-Tah

Map

Cartina

Kah R-TEE-Nah

Reservation

Prenotazione

PRĕ-NO-Tah-TSEE-Ó-Nĕ

Ticket

Biglietto

BEEL-Yĕ'T-TO

Tour

Viaggio / Gita

VEE-ah-JO / JEE-Tah

Tour guide

Guida turistica

GWEE-Dah TOO-REE'S-TEE-Kah

USEFUL PHRASES

Where is the tourist office?

Dov'è l'ufficio del turistico?

DŌ-VḖ LOO-FĒ-CHŌ DĒL

TOO-RĒS-TĒ-KŌ

Is there a tour to...?

Avete un giro turistico per...?

ah-VḖ-TḖ OON JĒ-RŌ

TOO-RĒS-TĒ-KŌ PĒR...

Where do I buy a ticket for...?

Dove posso comprare un biglietto per...

DŌ-VḖ PŌS-SŌ KOM-PRah-RḖ

OON BĒL-YḖ-TŌ PĒR...

How much does the tour cost?

Quanto costa il giro turistico?

KWah N-TŌ KŌS-Tah ĒL JĒ-RŌ

TOO-RĒS-TĒ-KŌ

How long does the tour take?

Quanto dura il giro turistico?

KWah N-TŌ DOO-Rah ĒL JĒ-RŌ

TOO-RĒS-TĒ-KŌ

Does the guide speak English?

La guida parla inglese?

L(ah) GW(EE)-D(ah) P(ah)R-L(ah) (EE)N-GL(A)-Z(A)

Are children free?

I bambini pagano?

(EE) B(ah)M-B(EE)-N(EE) P(ah)-G(ah)-N(O)

What time does the show start?

A che ora comincia lo spettacolo?

(ah) K(A) (O)-R(ah) K(O)-M(EE)N-CH(ah) L(O) SP(e)T-T(ah)-K(O)-L(O)

Do I need reservations?

E' necessaria la prenotazione?

(A) N(A)-CH(A)-S(ah)-R(EE)-(ah) L(ah) PR(A)-N(O)-T(ah)-TS(EE)-(O)-N(A)

Where can we go dancing?

Dove si può andare a ballare?

D(O)-V(A) S(EE) PW(O) (ah)N-D(ah)-R(A) (ah) B(ah)L-L(ah)-R(A)

Is there a minimum cover charge?

C'è un prezzo minimo?

CH(A) (oo)N PR(A)T-TS(O) M(EE)-N(EE)-M(O)

PHRASEMAKER

May I invite you...

Posso invitarti...

PⒶS-SⓄ   ⒺN-VⒺⒺ-TⓐⓇ-TⒺⒺ...

▶ **to a concert?**

a un concerto?

Ⓐ   ⓄⓄN   KⓄN-CHⒺⓇ-TⓄ

▶ **to dance?**

a ballare?

Ⓐ   BⒶL-LⒶ-RⒶ

▶ **to dinner?**

a pranzo?

Ⓐ   PRⒶN-TSⓄ

▶ **to the movies?**

al cinema?

ⒶL   CHⒺⒺ-NⒶ-MⒶ

▶ **to the theater?**

al teatro?

ⒶL   TⒶ-Ⓐ-TRⓄ

PHRASEMAKER

Where can I find...

Dove posso trovare...

DṒ-V℮ PṒS-SŌ TRŌ-V@h́-R℮...

▶ **a health club?**

un club ginnico?

ⓄN KLⓄ́B J℮N-N℮́-KŌ

▶ **a swimming pool?**

una piscina?

Ⓞ́-N@h P℮℮-SH℮℮́-N@h

▶ **a tennis court?**

un campo da tennis?

ⓄN K@h́M-PŌ D@h T℮́N-N℮℮S

▶ **a golf course?**

un campo di golf?

ⓄN K@h́M-PŌ D℮℮ GⓄLF

HEALTH

Hopefully you will not need medical attention on your trip. If you do, it is important to communicate basic information regarding your condition.

- Check with your insurance company before leaving home to find out if you are covered in a foreign country. You may want to purchase traveler's insurance before leaving home.

- If you take prescription medicine, carry your prescription with you. Have your prescriptions translated before you leave home.

- Take a small first-aid kit with you.

- Your embassy or consulate should be able to assist you in finding health care.

- Pharmacies are open in the morning and usually from 3:30 PM till 7:30 PM. A list of local pharmacies, open at night, is posted in the shop.

- Medical facilities and public hospitals are available in Italy. However, you may want to check your insurance for coverage for care or stay in a private Italian hospital or clinic.

KEY WORDS

Ambulance

Ambulanza

@M-B@-L@N-TS@

Dentist

Dentista

D@N-T@S-T@

Doctor

Medico

M@-D@-K@

Emergency!

Emergenza!

@-M@B-J@N-TS@

Hospital

Ospedale

@S-P@-D@-L@

Prescription

Ricetta

R@-CH@T-T@

USEFUL PHRASES

I am sick.

Sono ammalato. (male)   Sono ammalata. (female)

SÓ-NO ahM-Mah-Lah-TO (ah)

I need a doctor.

Ho bisogno di un dottore.

O BEE-ZÓN-YO DEE OON
DOT-TO-Rē

It's an emergency!

È un'emergenza!

ē OON ē-MēR-J̃ēN-Sah

Where is the nearest hospital?

Dov'è l'ospedale più vicino?

DO-Vē LOS-Pē-Dah-Lē PEE-oo
VEE-CHEE-NO

Call an ambulance!

Chiamate un'ambulanza!

KEE-ah-Mah-Tē OON ahM-Boo-Lah̃N-TSah

I'm allergic to...

Sono allergico a...

SŌ-NŌ ⓐL-Lⓔ́R-Jⓔ-KŌ ⓐ...

I'm pregnant.

Sono incinta.

SŌ-NŌ ⓔN-CHⓔ́N-Tⓐ

I'm diabetic.

Sono diabetico. (male) Sono diabetica. (female)

SŌ-NŌ Dⓔ-ⓐ-Bⓔ́-Tⓔ-KŌ (Kⓐ)

I have a heart condition.

Sono debole di cuore.

SŌ-NŌ Dⓔ́-BŌ-Lⓔ Dⓔ KWṒ-Rⓔ

I have high blood pressure.

Ho la pressione alta.

Ō Lⓐ PRⓔ́S-Sⓔ-Ṓ-Nⓔ ⓐ́L-Tⓐ

I have low blood pressure.

Ho la pressione bassa.

Ō Lⓐ PRⓔ́S-Sⓔ-Ṓ-Nⓔ Bⓐ́S-Sⓐ

PHRASEMAKER

I need…

Ho bisogno di...

Ⓞ BⒺⒺ-ZÓN-YⓄ DⒺⒺ…

▶ **a doctor**

un medico

ⓄⓄN Mⓔᷘᷘ-DⒺⒺ-KⓄ

▶ **a dentist**

un dentista

ⓄⓄN DⓔᷘN-TⒺⒺS-Tⓐⓗ

▶ **a nurse**

un'infermiera

ⓄⓄN ⒺⒺN-FⓔᷘR-MⒺⒺ-ⓔᷘ-Ⓡⓐⓗ

▶ **an optician**

un ottico

ⓄⓄN ⓄT-TⒺⒺ-KⓄ

▶ **a pharmacist**

un farmacista

ⓄⓄN FⓐⓗR-Mⓐⓗ-CHⒺⒺS-Tⓐⓗ

PHRASEMAKER

(AT THE PHARMACY)

Do you have...

Avete...

@-V@́-T@́...

▸ **aspirin?**

aspirina?

@S-P@-R@́-N@

▸ **Band-Aids?**

cerotti?

CH@-R@́T-T@

▸ **cough medicine?**

sciroppo per la tosse?

CH@-R@́P-P@ P@̋R L@ T@́S-S@

▸ **ear drops?**

gocce per le orecchi?

G@́-CH@ P@̋R L@ @-R@́-K@

▸ **eyedrops?**

collirio?

K@L-L@́-R@́-@

BUSINESS TRAVEL

It is important to show appreciation and interest in another person's language and culture, particularly when doing business. A few well-pronounced phrases can make a great impression.

I have an appointment.

Ho un appuntamento.

Ⓞ ⓄⓄN ⓐP-PⓄⓄN-Tⓐh-Mⓔ̃N-TⓄ

Here is my card.

Ecco il mio biglietto da visita.

Ⓔ̃K-KⓄ ⒺⒺL MⒺⒺ-Ⓞ BⒺⒺL-Yⓔ̃-TⓄ Dⓐh VⒺⒺ-ZⒺⒺ-Tⓐh

I need an interpreter?

Ho bisogno d'interprete?

Ⓞ BⒺⒺ-ZⓄ́N-YⓄ DⒺⒺN-Tⓔ̃R-PRⓐ-Tⓔ̃

May I speak to Mr....?

Posso parlare con il signor...?

PⓄ́S-SⓄ PⓐR-Lⓐh-RⒶ KⓄN ⒺⒺL SⒺⒺN-YⓄ́R...

May I speak to Mrs...?

Posso parlare con la signora...?

PⓄ́S-SⓄ PⓐR-Lⓐh-RⒶ KⓄN Lⓐh SⒺⒺN-YⓄ́-Rⓐh...

KEY WORDS

Appointment
Appuntamento
@P-P@N-T@-M@N-T@

Meeting
Incontro
@N-K@N-TR@

Marketing
Marketing
M@R-K@-T@N

Presentation
Presentazione
PR@-Z@N-T@-TS@-O-N@

Sales
Vendite
V@N-D@-T@

PHRASEMAKER

I need...

Ho bisogno di...

Ⓞ BⒺⒺ-ZⓄ'N-YⓄ DⒺⒺ...

▶ **a computer**

un computer

ⓄN KⓄM-PYⓄⓄ'-TⒺR

▶ **a copy machine**

una fotocopiatrice

ⓄⓄ'-Nⓐ FⓄ-TⓄ-KⓄ-PⒺⒺ-ⓐ-TRⒺⒺ'-CHⒶ

▶ **a conference room**

una sala conferenze

ⓄⓄ'-Nⓐ Sⓐⓑ'-Lⓐ KⓄN-FⒺ-RⒺN-TSⒺ

▶ **a fax machine**

una macchina per fax

ⓄⓄ'-Nⓐ Mⓐⓑ'-KⒺⒺ-Nⓐ PⒺR Fⓐ'KS

▶ **an interpreter**

un interprete

ⓄN ⒺⒺN-TⒺR-PRⒶ-TⒺ

▶ **a lawyer**

un avvocato

OON ahV-VO-Kah-TO

▶ **a notary**

un notaio

OON NO-Tah-YO

▶ **overnight delivery**

un recapito urgente

OON Reh-Kah-PEE-TO OOR-Jehn-TA

▶ **paper**

carta

Kah'R-Tah

▶ **a pen**

una penna

OO-Nah PAN-Nah

▶ **a pencil**

una matita

OO-Nah Mah-TEE-Tah

▶ **a secretary**

una segretaria

OO-Nah Sehg-Reh-Tah'R-Yah

GENERAL INFORMATION

From warm summers and cool winters in the north and hot summers and mild winters in southern Italy, there is something for everyone!

THE SEASONS

Spring

La primavera

Lah PREE-Mah-Vě-Rah

Summer

L'estate

Lě̆S-Tah́-Tě̆

Autumn

L'autunno

Low-TooN-No

Winter

L'inverno

Lee̊N-Vě̆R-No

THE DAYS

Monday
lunedì
L^{oo}-N^e-D^{EE}

Tuesday
martedì
M^{ah}R-T^e-D^{EE}

Wednesday
mercoledì
M^eR-K^O-L^e-D^{EE}

Thursday
giovedì
J^O-V^e-D^{EE}

Friday
venerdì
V^e-N^eR-D^{EE}

Saturday
sabato
S^{ah}-B^{ah}-T^O

Sunday
domenica
D^O-M^e-N^{EE}-K^{ah}

THE MONTHS

January
gennaio
JĔN-Nah-YO

February
febbraio
FĔB-BRah-YO

March
marzo
Mah-RTSO

April
aprile
ah-PREE-Lĕ

May
maggio
Mah-JO

June
giugno
JooN-YO

July
luglio
LooL-YO

August
agosto
ah-GOS-TO

September
settembre
SĔT-TĕM-BRĕ

October
ottobre
OT-TO-BRĕ

November
novembre
NO-VĕM-BRĕ

December
dicembre
DEE-CHĕM-BRĕ

COLORS

Black	**White**
Nero	Bianco
NĒ-RO	BEE-ahN-KO
Blue	**Brown**
Blu	Marrone
BLoo	Mah-RO-NĒ
Gray	**Gold**
Grigio	Oro
GREE-JO	O-RO
Orange	**Yellow**
Arancione	Giallo
ah-RahN-CHO-NĒ	GEE-ahL-LO
Red	**Green**
Rosso	Verde
RO'S-SO	VĒR-DĒ
Pink	**Purple**
Rosa	Porpora
RO-Sah	PO'R-PO-Rah

NUMBERS

0	1	2
zero	uno	due
TSĕ-RO	ōō-NO	Dōō-ĕ

3	4	5
tre	quattro	cinque
TRĕ	KWah-T-TRO	CHēēN-KWĕ

6	7	8
sei	sette	otto
Sĕēē	Sĕ'T-Tĕ	ōT-TO

9	10	11
nove	dieci	undici
NŌ-Vĕ	Dēē-ĕ-CHēē	ōōN-Dēē-CHēē

12	13
dodici	tredici
DO-Dēē-CHēē	TRĕ-Dēē-CHēē

14	15
quattordici	quindici
KWah-T-TOB-Dēē-CHēē	KWēēN-Dēē-CHēē

16	17
sedici	diciassette
Sĕ-Dēē-CHēē	Dēē-CHahS-Sĕ'T-Tĕ

18

diciotto

DEE-CHŌT-TO

19

diciannove

DEE-CHah-N-NŌ-Vĕ

20

venti

VĕN-TEE

30

trenta

TRĕN-Tah

40

quaranta

KWah-Rah-N-Tah

50

cinquanta

CHEEN-KWah-N-Tah

60

sessanta

Sĕ-Sah-N-Tah

70

settanta

SĕT-Tah-N-Tah

80

ottanta

OT-Tah-N-Tah

90

novanta

NO-Vah-N-Tah

100

cento

CHĕN-TO

1000

mille

MEEL-Lĕ

1,000,000

milione

MEEL-YŌ-Nĕ

DICTIONARY

Each English entry is followed
by the Italian word and then the
EPLS Vowel Symbol System.
Gender of nouns and adjectives
is indicated by (m) for masculine
and (f) for feminine.

A

a, an un, uno ⓞⓞN ⓞⓞ-Nⓞ

a lot molto MⓞL-Tⓞ

able (to be) potere Pⓞ-Tⓔ-Rⓔ

above sopra Sⓞ-PRⓐ

accident incidente ⒺN-CHⒺ-DⓔN-Tⓔ

accommodation sistemazione

    SⒺS-Tⓔ-Mⓐ-TSⒺ-Ⓞ-Nⓔ

account conto KⓞN-Tⓞ

address indirizzo ⒺN-DⒺ-RⒺT-TSⓞ

admission ingresso ⒺN-GRⓔS-Sⓞ

afraid (to be) aver paura ⓐ-VⓔR Pⓐ-ⓞⓞ-Rⓐ

after dopo Dⓞ-Pⓞ

afternoon pomeriggio Pⓞ-Mⓔ-RⒺ-Jⓞ

air conditioning aria condizionata

    ⓐ-RⒺ-ⓐ KⓞN-DⒺ-TSⒺ-Ⓞ-Nⓐ-Tⓐ

aircraft aereo ah-é-Ré-O

airline compagnia aerea

KOM-Pah-NEE-ah ah-é-Ré-ah

airport aeroporto ah-é-RO-POR-TO

aisle corridoio KO-REE-DO-EE-O

all tutto TooT-TO

almost quasi KWah-ZEE

alone solo SO-LO

also anche ahN-Ké

always sempre SéM-PRé

ambulance ambulanza ahM-Boo-LahN-TSah

America americano ah-Mé-REE-Kah

American americano ah-Mé-REE-Kah-NO

americana ah-Mé-REE-Kah-Nah

and e é

another un altro ooN ahL-TRO

anything qualsiasi cosa KWahL-SEE-ah-SEE KO-Sah

apartment appartamento ahP-Pah-R-Tah-MéN-TO

appetizers antipasti ahN-TEE-Pah-S-TEE

apple mela Mé-Lah

appointment appuntamento ahP-PooN-Tah-MéN-TO

April aprile ⓐ-PRⒺⒺ-Lⓔ

arrival arrivo ⓐ-RⒺⒺ-Vⓞ

arrive (to) arrivare ⓐ-RⒺⒺ-Vⓐ-Rⓔ

ashtray portacenere PⓄR-Tⓐ-CHⓔ-Nⓔ-Rⓔ

aspirin aspirina ⓐS-PⒺⒺ-RⒺⒺ-Nⓐ

attention attenzione ⓐT-TⓔN-TSⒺⒺ-Ⓞ-Nⓔ

August agosto ⓐ-GⓄS-Tⓞ

Australia Australia ⓄⓌ-STRⒶ-LⒺⒺ-ⓐ

Australian Australiano (m) ⓄⓌ-STRⓐ-LⒺⒺ-ⓐ-Nⓞ

Australiana (f) ⓄⓌ-STRⓐ-LⒺⒺ-ⓐ-Nⓐ

author autore ⓄⓌ-Tⓞ-Rⓔ

automobile macchina Mⓐ-KⒺⒺ-Nⓐ

autumn autunno ⓄⓌ-TⓄⓄN-Nⓞ

avenue corso KⓄR-Sⓞ

awful terribile TⓔR-RⒺⒺ-BⒺⒺ-LⓔY

B

baby bambino BⓐM-BⒺⒺ-Nⓞ

babysitter babysitter Bⓔ-BⒺⒺ-SⒺⒺ-TⓔR

bacon pancetta PⓐN-CHⓔT-Tⓐ

bad cattivo KⓐT-TⒺⒺ-Vⓞ

bag borsa BOR-Sah

baggage bagaglio Bah-GahL-YO

baked al forno ahL FOR-NO

bakery (bread) panetteria Pah-NeT-Te-Ree-ah

banana banana Bah-Nah-Nah

Band-Aid cerotto CHe-ROT-TO

bank banca BahN-Kah

barbershop barbiere BahB-Bee-e-Re

bartender barista Bah-ReeS-Tah

bath bagno BahN-YO

bathing suit costume da bagno
KOS-Too-Me Dah BahN-YO

bathroom bagno BahN-YO

battery batteria BahT-Te-Ree-ah

beach spiaggia SPee-ah-Jah

beautiful bellissimo BeL-LeeS-See-MO

beauty shop salone di belleza
Sah-LO-Ne Dee BeL-LeT-Sah

bed letto LeT-TO

beef manzo MahN-TSO

beer birra Bee-Bah

bellman fattorino FⓐT-TⓄ-RⒺⒺ-NⓄ

belt cintura CHⒺⒺN-TⓄⓄ-Rⓐ

big grande GRⓐN-DⒺ

bill conto KⓄN-TⓄ

black nero NⒺ-RⓄ

blanket coperta KⓄ-PⒺR-Tⓐ

blue blu BLⓄⓄ

boat barca BⓐR-Kⓐ

book libro LⒺⒺ-BRⓄ

bookstore libreria LⒺⒺ-BRⒺ-RⒺⒺ-ⓐ

border confine KⓄN-FⒺⒺ-NⒺ

boy ragazzo Rⓐ-Gⓐ T-TSⓄ

bracelet bracciale BRⓐ-CHⒺⒺ-ⓐ-LⒺ

brakes freni FRⒺ-NⒺⒺ

bread pane Pⓐ-NⒺ

breakfast colazione KⓄ-Lⓐ-TSⒺⒺ-Ⓞ-NⒺ

broiled alla griglia ⓐL-Lⓐ GRⒺⒺL-Yⓐ

brown marrone Mⓐ-RⓄ-NⒺ

brush spazzola SPⓐT-TSⓄ-Lⓐ

building edificio Ⓔ-DⒺⒺ-FⒺⒺ-CHⓄ

bus autobus ⓄⓌ-TⓄ-BⓄⓄS

bus station stazione dell'autobus

STAH-TSEE-O'-NE DEL OW-TO-BOOS

bus stop fermata dell'autobus

FER-MAH-TAH DEL OW-TO-BOOS

business affari AHF-FAH-REE

butter burro BOO-RO

buy (to) comprare KOM-PRAH-RE

C

cab tassì TAH-SEE

call (to) chiamare KEE-AH-MAH-RE

camera macchina fotografica

MAH-KEE-NAH FO-TO-GRAH-FEE-KAH

Canada Canada KAH'-NAH-DAH

Canadian Canadese KAH'-NAH-DE'-ZE

candy caramella KAH-RAH-MEL-LAH

car auto OW'-TO

carrot carota KAH-RO'-TAH

castle castello KAHS-TEL-LO

cathedral cattedrale KAH-TE-DRAH-LE

celebration celebrazione CHE-LE-BRAH-TSEE-O'-NE

center centro CHEN-TRO

cereal cereali CH&-R&-@h-L&

chair sedia S&-D&-@h

champagne champagne SH@M-P@N-Y@

change (to) cambiare K@M-B&-@h-R&

cheap a buon mercato @h BW@N M&R-K@h-T@

check (bill in a restaurant) conto K@N-T@

cheers salute S@h-L@-T&

cheese formaggio F@R-M@h-J@

chicken pollo P@L-L@

child bambino B@M-B&-N@

chocolate (flavor) cioccolata CH@K-K@-L@h-T@h

church chiesa K&-&-S@h

cigar sigaro S&-G@h-R@

cigarettes sigarette S&-G@h-R&T-T&

city città CH&T-T@h

clean pulito P@-L&-T@

close (to) chiudere K&-@-D&-R&

closed chiuso K&-@-Z@

clothes vestiti V&S-T&-T&

cocktail cocktail K@K-T&L

coffee caffé K@h-F&

cold (temperature) freddo FREHD-DO

comb pettine PEHT-TEE-NEH

come (to) venire VEH-NEE-REH

company (business) ditta DEET-Tah

computer computer KOM-PYOO-TEHR

concert concerto KON-CHEHR-TO

condom preservativo PREH-SEHR-Vah-TEE-VO

conference conferenza KON-FEH-REHN-TSah

conference room sala conferenze

　　Sah-Lah KON-FEH-REHN-TSEH

congratulations congratulazioni

　　KON-GRah-TOO-Lah-TSEE-O-NEE

copy machine fotocopiatrice

　　FO-TO-KO-PEE-ah-TREE-CHEH

corn granturco GRahN-TOOR-KO

cough medicine sciroppo per la tosse

　　SHEER-OP-O PEHR Lah TOS-SEH

cover charge coperto KO-PEHR-TO

crab granchio GRahN-KEE-O

cream crema KREH-Mah

credit card carta di credito

    KⓐR-Tⓐ DⒺⒺ KRⒺ-DⒺⒺ-TⓄ

cup tazza Tⓐ-TSⓐ

customs dogana DⓄ-Gⓐ-Nⓐ

D

dance (to) ballare BⓐL-Lⓐ-RⒺ

dangerous pericoloso PⒺ-RⒺ-KⓄ-LⓄ-SⓄ

date (calendar) data Dⓐ-Tⓐ

day giorno JⒺⒺ-ⓄR-NⓄ

December dicembre DⒺⒺ-CHⒺM-BRⒺ

delicious delizioso DⒺ-LⒺⒺ-TSⒺⒺ-Ⓞ-SⓄ

delighted lietissimo LⒺⒺ-Ⓔ-TⒺⒺ-SⒺⒺ-MⓄ

dentist dentista DⒺN-TⒺⒺS-Tⓐ

deodorant deodorante DⒺ-Ⓞ-DⓄ-Rⓐ N-TⒺ

department store grande magazzino

    GRⓐN-DⒺ Mⓐ-Gⓐ-TSⒺⒺ-NⓄ

departure partenza PⓐR-TⒺN-TSⓐ

dessert dolce DⓄL-CHⒺ

detour deviazione DⒺ-VⒺⒺ-ⓐ-TSⒺⒺ-Ⓞ-NⒺ

diabetic diabetico DⒺⒺ-ⓐ-BⒺ-TⒺⒺ-KⓄ

diarrhea diarrea DⒺⒺ-ⓐ-RⒺ-ⓐ

dictionary dizionario DEE-TSEE-O-Nah-REE-O

dinner cena CHĕ-Nah

dining room sala da pranzo

    Sah-Lah Dah PRah́N-TSO

directions indicazioni EEN-DEE-Kah-TSEE-O-NEE

dirty sporco SPO͞R-KO

disabled invalido EEN-Vah́-LEE-DO

discount sconto SKO͞N-TO

distance distanza DEES-Tah́N-TSah

doctor dottore DOT-TO͞-Rĕ

document documento DO-Koo-MĕN-TO

dollar dollaro DO͞L-Lah-RO

down giú Joo

downtown in centro EEN CHĕN-TRO

dress vestito VĕS-TĔ-TO

drink (to) bere Bĕ́-Rĕ

drive (to) guidare GWEE-Dah́-Rĕ

drugstore farmacia Fah́R-Mah-CHEE-ah

dry cleaner lavanderia a secco

    Lah-Vah́N-Dĕ-Rĕ́-ah ah Sĕ́K-KO

duck anitra ah́-NEE-TRah

E

ear orecchio Ⓞ-Ⓡⓔ́-ⓀⒺⒺ-Ⓞ

ear drops gocce per le orecchie

    GⓄ́-CHⓔ PⓐⓇ Lⓔ Ⓞ-Ⓡⓔ́-ⓀⒺⒺ-ⓔ

early presto PRⓔ́S-TⓄ

east est ⓔST

easy facile Fⓐ́-CHⒺⒺ-Lⓔ

eat (to) mangiare Mⓐ́N-Jⓐ́-Rⓔ

eggs (fried) uova fritte WⓄ́-Vⓐ FRⒺⒺT-Tⓔ

eggs (scrambled) uova strapazzate

    WⓄ́-Vⓐ STRⓐ-Pⓐ-TSⓐ́-Tⓔ

eggs uova WⓄ́-Vⓐ

electricity corrente KⓄ-Rⓔ́N-Tⓔ

elevator ascensore ⓐ-SHⓔ́N-SⓄ-Rⓔ

embassy ambasciata ⓐM-Bⓐ-SHⓐ́-Tⓐ

emergency emergenza ⓔ-Mⓔ́R-Jⓔ́N-TSⓐ

England Inghilteria ⒺⒺN-GⒺⒺL-Tⓔ́R-ⒺⒺ-ⓤⓗ

English inglese ⒺⒺN-GLⓔ́-Zⓔ

enough basta Bⓐ́S-Tⓐ

entrance ingresso ⒺⒺN-GRⓔ́S-SⓄ

envelope busta BⓄⓄ́S-Tⓐ

evening sera Sĕ'-Rah

everything tutto TⓞⓞT-Tⓞ

excellent eccellente ĕ-CHĕL-Lĕ'N-Tĕ

excuse me mi scusi Mĕ SKⓞⓞ'-Zĕ

exit uscita ⓞⓞ-SHĕ'-Tah

expensive caro Kah'-Rⓞ

eyedrops gocce per gli occhi

    Gⓞ'-CHĕ Pĕ'R LYĕ ⓞ'K-Kĕ

eyes occhi ⓞ'K-Kĕ

F

face faccia Fah'-CHah

far lontano LⓞN-Tah'-Nⓞ

fare (cost) costo Kⓞ'S-Tⓞ

fast veloce Vĕ-Lⓞ'-CHĕ

fax machine macchina per fax

    Mah'K-Kĕ-Nah Pĕ'R Fah'KS

February febbraio Fĕ'B-BRah'-Yⓞ

few alcuni ah'L-Kⓞⓞ'-Nĕ

film (movie) rull RⓞⓞL

film (camera) rullino RⓞⓞL-Lĕ'-Nⓞ

fine (very well) bene Bĕ'-Nĕ

finger dito DEE-TO

fire extinguisher estintore ES-TEEN-TO-RE

fire fuoco FWO-KO

first primo PREE-MO

fish pesce PE-SHE

flight volo VO-LO

florist shop fiorista FEE-O-REES-Tah

flower fiore FEE-O-RE

food cibo CHEE-BO

foot piede PEE-E-DE

fork forchetta FOR-KET-Tah

french fries patatine fritte

    Pah-Tah-TEE-NE FREET-TE

fresh fresco FRES-KO

Friday venerdì VE-NER-DEE

fried fritto FREET-TO

friend amico ahM-EE-KO

fruit frutta FROOT-Tah

funny divertente DEE-VER-TEN-TE

G

gas station distributore DEES-TREE-BOO-TO-RE

gasoline benzina BEN-TSEE-Nah

gate cancello KahN-CHEL-LO

gentleman signore SEEN-YO-RE

gift regalo RE-Gah-LO

girl ragazza Rah-GahT-TSah

glass (drinking) bicchiere BEEK-YE-RE

glasses (eye) occhiali OK-KEE-ah-LEE

gloves guanti GWahN-TEE

go forza FOR-TSah

gold oro O-RO

golf course campo di golf KahM-PO DEE GOLF

golf golf GOLF

good buono BWO-NO

good-bye arrivederci ah-REE-VE-DER-CHE

goose oca O-Kah

grapes uva OO-Vah

grateful grato GRah-TO

gray grigio GREE-JO

green verde VER-DE

grocery store drogheria DR̄O-G̈ë-R̈Eë́-ah

group gruppo GR̄oõP-PO

guide guida GWëÉ-Dah

H

hair capelli Kah-P̈ëL-L̄Eë

hairbrush spazzola SPahT-TSO-Lah

haircut taglio di capelli

    TahL-YO Dëë Kah-P̈ëL-L̄Eë

ham prosciutto PR̄O-SHoõT-TO

hamburger hamburger ahM-BoṍR-G̈ëR̄

hand mano Mah́-NO

happy felice / contento

    Fë-L̄Eë́-CHë / KON-T̈ëN-TO

have, I ho O

he lui Loṍ-ëë

head testa T̈ëS-Tah

headache mal di testa Mah̄L Dëë T̈ëS-Tah

health club club ginnico KLoõB J̈ëN-N̈Eë́-KO

heart cuore KWO̊́-R̄ë

heart condition debole di cuore

    D̈ë́-BO-L̄ë Dëë KWO̊́-R̄ë

heat calore Kah-LO-Re

hello ciao CHow

help aiuto ah-Yoo-TO

here qui KWee

holiday vacanza Vah-Kah-Zah

hospital ospedale OS-Pe-Dah-Le

hot dog hot dog ahT Dah G

hotel hotel O-TeL

hour ora O-Rah

how come KO-Me

hurry up sbrigarsi ZBRee-Gah R-See

I

I io ee-O

ice ghiaccio Gee-ah-CHO

ice cream gelato Je-Lah-TO

ice cubes cubetti di ghiaccio
    Koo-Be T-Tee Dee Gee-ah-CHO

ill ammalato ahM-Mah-Lah-TO

important importante eeM-POR-Tah N-Te

indigestion indigestione eeN-Dee-Je S-Tee-O-Ne

information informazione eeN-FOR-Mah-TSee-O-Ne

inn albergo ⓐL-ⒷⒺⓇ-Gⓞ

interpreter interprete ⒺN-TⒺⓇ-PⓇⒺ-TⒺ

J

jacket giubbotto Jⓞⓞ-ⒷⓄ'T-Tⓞ

jam marmellata Mⓐ'Ⓡ-MⒺL-Lⓐ'-Tⓐ

January gennaio JⒺN-Nⓐ'-Yⓞ

jewelry gioielli Jⓞ-YⒺ'L-LⒺⒺ

jewelry store gioielleria Jⓞ-YⒺL-LⒺ-ⓇⒺⒺ-ⓐ

job lavoro Lⓐ'-VⓄ'-Ⓡⓞ

juice succo SⓞⓞK-Kⓞ

July luglio Lⓞⓞ'L-Yⓞ

June giugno Jⓞⓞ'N-Yⓞ

K

ketchup ketchup KⒺ'-CHⓞⓞP

key chiave KⒺⒺ-ⓐ'-VⒺ

kiss bacio Bⓐ'-CHⓞ

knife coltello KⓄL-TⒺ'L-Lⓞ

know (to) sapere Sⓐ-PⒺ'-ⓇⒺ

L

ladies' restroom toilette per le donne

TWah-LĚT PĚR LĚ DŎN-NĚ

lady signora SĒN-YŎ-Bah

lamb agnello ahN-YĚL-LŎ

language lingua LĒN-GWah

large grande GBahN-DĚ

late tardi TahB-DĒ

laundry lavanderia Lah-Vah-N-DĚ-BĒ-ah

lawyer avvocato ahV-VŎ-Kah-TŎ

left (direction) sinistra SĒ-NĒS-TBah

leg gamba GahM-Bah

lemon limone LĒ-MŎ-NĚ

less meno MĚ-NŎ

letter lettera LĚT-TĚ-Bah

lettuce lattuga Lah-TŌŌ-Gah

light luce LŌŌ-CHĚ

like (to) piacere PĒ-ah-CHĚ-BĚ

like (I would) vorrei VŎ-BĚ-Ē

lip labbro LahB-BBŎ

lipstick rossetto BŎS-SĚT-TŎ

little piccolo PEEK-KO-LO

little poco PO-KO

live (to) vivere VEE-Vē-Bē

lobster aragosta ah-Bah-GOS-Tah

long lungo LooN-GO

lost perduto PēB-Doo-TO

love amore ah-MO-Bē

luck fortuna FOB-Too-Nah

luggage bagaglio Bah-Gah-L-YO

lunch pranzo PBahN-TSO

M

maid cameriera Kah-Mē-Bēē-ē-Bah

mail posta POS-Tah

makeup trucco TBooK-KO

man uomo WO-MO

manager direttore DEE-Bēt-TO-Bē

map cartina KahB-TEE-Nah

March marzo MahB-TSO

market mercato MēB-Kah-TO

matches fiammiferi FEE-ah M-MEE-Fē-Bēē

May maggio Mah-JO

mayonnaise maionese Mah-YO-Ne-Se

meal pasto Pah'S-TO

meat carne Kah'B-Ne

mechanic meccanico Me-Kah-Nee-KO

medicine medicina Me-Dee-CHee-Nah

meeting incontro een-KON-TBO

mens' restroom toilette per uomini
    TWah-Le'T Peb WO-Mee-Nee

menu menù Me-Noo

message messaggio MeS-Sah'-JO

milk latte Lah'T-Te

mineral water acqua minerale ah'-KWah
    Mee-Ne-Bah-Le

minute minuto Mee-Noo'-TO

Miss Signorina Seen-YO-Bee-Nah

mistake sbaglio SBah'L-YO

misunderstanding malinteso Mah-Leen-Te'-SO

moment momento MO-Me'N-TO

Monday lunedì Loo-Ne-Dee

money soldi SOL-Dee

month mese Me'-Se

monument monumento MO-No-MĒN-TO

more piú PĒ-oó

morning mattina Mah-T-TĒ-Nah

mosque moschea MOS-KĒ-ah

mother madre Mah-DRĒ

mountain montagna MON-Tah-N-Yah

movies film FēLM

Mr. Signore SēN-YO-Rē

Mrs. Signora SēN-YO-Rah

much, too molto MOL-TO

museum museo Moo-Sē-O

mushrooms funghi Foo-N-Gē

music musica Moo-Sē-Kah

mustard senape Sē-Nah-Pē

N

nail polish smalto per le unghie

    SMah-L-TO PēR Lē oo-N-Gē

name nome NO-Mē

napkin tovagliolo TO-Vah-L-YO-LO

near vicino Vē-CHē-NO

neck collo KO-L-LO

need, I ho bisogno Ⓞ BⒺⒺ-ZⓄN-YⓄ

never mai Mⓐⓗ-ⒺⒺ

newspaper giornale JⓄⓇ-Nⓐⓗ-LⒺ

news stand edicola Ⓔ-DⒺⒺ-KⓄ-Lⓐⓗ

next time la prossima volta

    Lⓐⓗ PⓇⓄS-SⒺⒺ-Mⓐⓗ VⓄL-Tⓐⓗ

night notte NⓄT-TⒺ

nightclub locale notturno

    LⓄ-Kⓐⓗ-LⒺ NⓄT-TⓄⓄⓇ-NⓄ

no no NⓄ

no smoking non fumatori NⓄN FⓄⓄ-Mⓐⓗ-TⓄ-ⓇⒺⒺ

noon mezzogiorno MⒺ-TSⓄ-JⓄⓇ-NⓄ

north nord NⓄⓇD

notary notaio NⓄ-Tⓐⓗ-YⓄ

November novembre NⓄ-VⒺM-BⓇⒺ

now adesso ⓐⓗ-DⒺS-SⓄ

number numero NⓄⓄ-MⒺ-ⓇⓄ

nurse infermiera ⒺⒺN-FⒺⓇ-MⒺⒺ-Ⓔ-Ⓡⓐⓗ

O

occupied occupato ⓄK-KⓄⓄ-Pⓐⓗ-TⓄ

ocean oceano Ⓞ-CHⒺ-ⓐⓗ-NⓄ

October ottobre ⓞT-TⓄ-BBⓔ

officer ufficiale ⓞⓞF-FⒺ-CHⓐⓗ-Lⓔ

oil olio ⓄL-YⓄ

omelet frittata FBⒺT-Tⓐⓗ-Tⓐⓗ

one-way (traffic) senso unico SⓔN-SⓄ ⓞⓞ-NⒺ-KⓄ

onions cipolle CHⒺ-PⓄL-Lⓔ

open (to) aprire ⓐⓗ-PBⒺ-Bⓔ

opera opera Ⓞ-Pⓔ-Bⓐⓗ

operator centralinista CHⓔN-TBⓐⓗ-LⒺ-NⒺS-Tⓐⓗ

optician ottico ⓞT-TⒺ-KⓄ

orange arancione ⓐⓗ-BⓐⓗN-CHⓄ-NⒶ

orange (fruit) arancia ⓐⓗ-BⓐⓗN-CHⓐⓗ

order (to) ordinare ⓞB-DⒺ-Nⓐⓗ-Bⓔ

original originale Ⓞ-BⒺ-JⒺ-Nⓐⓗ-Lⓔ

owner proprietario PBⓄ-PBⒺ-ⓔ-Tⓐⓗ-BⒺ-Ⓞ

oyster ostriche ⓄS-TBⒺ-Kⓔ

P

package pacco PⓐⓗK-KⓄ

paid pagato Pⓐⓗ-Gⓐⓗ-TⓄ

pain dolore DⓄ-LⓄ-Bⓔ

painting dipinto DⒺ-PⓔN-TⓄ

pantyhose collant KOL-L@NT

paper carta K@B-T@

park (to) parcheggiare P@B-K@-J@-B@

park parco P@B-K@

partner (business) socio S@-CH@

party festa F@S-T@

passenger passeggero P@S-S@-J@-B@

passport passaporto P@S-S@-P@B-T@

pasta pasta P@S-T@

pastry shop pasticcini P@S-T@-CH@-N@

pen penna P@N-N@

pencil matita M@-T@-T@

pepper pepe P@-P@

perfume profumo P@-F@-M@

person persona P@B-S@-N@

person to person diretta con preavviso
    D@-B@T-T@ K@N P@-@-V@-Z@

pharmacist un farmacista @N F@B-M@-CH@S-T@

pharmacy farmacia F@B-M@-CH@-@

phone book elenco telefonica
    @-L@N-K@ T@-L@-F@-N@-K@

photo foto FŌ-TŌ

photographer fotografo FŌ-TŌ-GRah-FŌ

pie or cake torta TŌR-Tah

pillow cuscino Koo-SHEE-NŌ

pink rosa RŌ-Sah

pizza pizza PEET-Sah

plastic plastica PLahS-TEE-Kah

plate piatto PEE-ahT-TŌ

please per favore / per piacere

     PĒR Fah-VŌ-Rē / PĒR PEE-ah-CHē-Rē

pleasure piacere PEE-ah-CHē-Rē

police polizia PŌ-LEE-TSEE-ah

police station stazione di polizia

     STah-TSEE-Ō-Nē DEE PŌ-LEE-TSEE-ah

pork maiale Mah-Yah-Lē

porter facchino Fah-KEE-NŌ

post office ufficio postale

     oo-FEE-CHŌ PŌS-Tah-Lē

postcard cartolina Kah-R-TŌ-LEE-Nah

potato patata Pah-Tah-Tah

pregnant incinta EEN-CHEEN-Tah

prescription ricetta REE-CHET-Tah

price prezzo PREE-TSO

problem problema PRO-BLEE-Mah

profession professione PRO-FES-SEE-O-NE

public pubblico POOB-BLEE-KO

public telephone telefono pubblico
TE-LE-FO-NO POOB-BLEE-KO

purified purificata POO-REE-FEE-Kah-Tah

purple porpora POR-PO-Rah

purse borsetta BOR-SET-Tah

Q

quality qualità KWah-LEE-Tah

question domanda DO-Mah'N-Dah

quickly in fretta EN FRET-Tah

quiet! quieto! KWEE-E-TO

quiet (to be) zitto SEET-TO

R

radio radio Rah-DEE-O

railroad ferrovia FER-O-VEE-ah

rain pioggia PEE-O-Jah

raincoat impermeabile EEM-PER-MEE-ah-BEE-LE

ramp rampa RahM-Pah

rare (steak) al sangue ahL SahN-GWE

razor blades lamette Lah-MET-TE

ready pronto PRON-TO

receipt ricevuta REE-CHE-VOO-Tah

recommend (to) raccomandare

    RahK-KO-MahN-Dah-RE

red rosso ROS-SO

repeat ripeta REE-PE-Tah

reservation prenotazione PRE-NO-Tah-TSEE-O-NE

restaurant ristorante REES-TO-RahN-TE

return (to come back) ritornare REE-TOR-Nah-RE

return (to give back) restituire RES-TEE-TOO-EE-RE

rice riso REE-ZO

rich ricco REEK-KO

right (correct) giusto JOOS-TO

right (direction) destra DES-TRah

road strada STRah-Dah

room stanza STahN-TSah

round trip andata e ritorno

    ahN-Dah-Tah ē RēE-TOR-NO

S

safe (box) cassaforte KahS-Sah-FOR-Tē

salad insalata ēEN-Sah-Lah-Tah

sale vendita VēN-DēE-Tah

salmon salmone SahL-MON-ē

salt sale Sah-Lē

sandwich panino Pah-NēE-NO

Saturday sabato Sah-Bah-TO

scissors forbici FOR-BēE-CHēE

sculpture scultura SKooL-Too-Rah

seafood frutti di mare FRoo-Tē Dē Mah-Rē

season stagione STah-JO-Nē

seat posto POS-TO

secretary segretario SēG-Rē-Tah-RY-O

section sezione Sē-TSēE-O-Nē

September settembre SēT-TēM-BRē

service servizio SēR-Vē-TSēE-O

several diversi Dē-VēR-Sē

shampoo shampoo SH@M-P◎

sheets (bed) lenzuola L©N-TSW◎-L@

shirt camicia K@-M©-CH@

shoe scarpa SK@B-P@

shoe store negozio di scarpe

N©-G◎-TS©-◎ D© SK@B-P©

shop (store) negozio N©-G◎-TS©-◎

shopping center centro commerciale

CH©N-TB◎ K◎-M©B-CH©-@-L©

shower doccia D◎-CH@

shrimp gamberetti G@M-B©-B©T-T©

sick malato M@-L@-T◎

sign (display) cartello K@B-T©L-L◎

signature firma F©B-M@

single singolo S©N-G◎-L◎

sir signore S©N-Y◎-B©

sister sorella S◎-B©L-L@

size taglia T@L-Y@

skin pelle P©L-L©

skirt gonna G◎N-N@

sleeve manica M@N-N©-K@

slowly lentamente LEN-Tah-MEN-Te

small piccolo PEEK-KO-LO

smile (to) sorridere SOR-REE-DE-RE

smoke (to) fumare FOO-MAH-RE

soap sapone Sah-PON-E

sock calza KahL-TSah

some qualche KWahL-KE

something qualcosa KWahL-KO-Zah

sometimes a volta ah VOL-Tah

soon presto PRES-TO

sorry (I am) mi dispiace MEE DEES-PEE-ah-CHE

soup minestra MEE-NES-TRah

south sud SOOD

souvenir ricordo REE-KOR-DO

Spanish spagnolo SPahN-YO-LO

speciality specialità SPE-CHEE-ah-LEE-Tah

speed velocità VE-LO-CHEE-Tah

spoon cucchiaio KOOK-Yah-YO

sport sport SPORT

spring primavera PREE-Mah-VE-Rah

stairs scale SKah-LE

stamp francobollo FR@hN-K⦵-B⦵'L-L⦵

station stazione ST@h-TS㋐-⦵'-N㋐

steak bistecca B㋐S-T㋐'-K@h

steamed al vapore @hL V@h-P⦵'-R㋐

stop si fermi S㋐ F㋐'R-M㋐

store negozio N㋐-G⦵'-TS㋐-⦵

storm temporale T㋐M-P⦵-R@h'-L㋐

straight ahead avanti diritto

    @h-V@h'N-T㋐ D㋐-R㋐'T-T⦵

strawberry fragola FR@h'-G⦵-L@h

street via V㋐'-@h

string corda K⦵'R-D@h

subway metropolitana M㋐-TR⦵-P⦵-L㋐-T@h'-N@h

sugar zucchero TS⦵⦵'K-K㋐-R⦵

suit (clothes) abito completo

    @h-B㋐'-T⦵ K⦵M-PL㋐'-T⦵

suitcase valigia V@h-L㋐'-CH@h

summer estate ㋐S-T@h'-T㋐

sun sole S⦵'-L㋐

Sunday domenica D⦵-M㋐'-N㋐-K@h

sunglasses occhiali da sole

ⓄK-Kㄸ-ⓐí-Lㄸ Dⓐ SⓄ́-Lⓔ̃

suntan lotion crema solare KRⓔ̃-Mⓐ SⓄ-Lⓐ́-Rⓔ̃

supermarket supermercato Sⓞⓞ-Pⓔ̃R-Mⓔ̃R-Kⓐ́-TⓄ

surprise sorpresa SⓄR-PRⓔ̃́-Zⓐ

sweet dolce DⓄ́L-CHⓔ̃

swim (to) nuotare NWⓄ-Tⓐ́-Rⓔ̃

swimming pool piscina Pㄸ-SHㄸ́-Nⓐ

synagogue sinagoga Sㄸ-Nⓐ-GⓄ́-Gⓐ

T

table tavola Tⓐ́-VⓄ-Lⓐ

tampons tamponi Tⓐ́M-PⓄ́-Nㄸ

tape (sticky) nastro adesivo

Nⓐ́S-TRⓄ ⓐ-Dⓔ̃-Sㄸ́-VⓄ

tape recorder registratore Rⓔ̃-Jㄸ-STRⓐ́-TⓄ́-Rⓔ̃

tax imposta ㄸM-PⓄ́S-Tⓐ

taxi tassì Tⓐ́-Sㄸ

tea tè Tⓔ̃

telegram telegramma Tⓔ̃-Lⓔ̃-GRⓐ́M-Mⓐ

telephone telefono Tⓔ̃-Lⓔ̃́-FⓄ-NⓄ

television televisione Tⓔ̃-Lⓔ̃-Vㄸ-Sㄸ-Ⓞ́-Nⓔ̃

temperature temperatura TⓔM-PⓔR-ⓐ-TⓄⓄ-Rⓐ

temple tempio TⓔM-PⒺⒺ-Ⓞ

tennis tennis TⓔN-NⒺⒺS

tennis court campo da tennis

    KⓐM-PⓄ Dⓐ TⓔN-NⒺⒺS

thank you molte grazie MⓄL-Tⓔ GRⓐ-TSⒺⒺ-ⓔ

that quello KWⓔL-LⓄ

the il / la / l' / i / gli / le ⒺⒺL / Lⓐ / LⓄ /

    ⒺⒺ / LYⒺⒺ / Lⓔ

theater teatro Tⓔ-ⓐ-TRⓄ

there là Lⓐ

they loro LⓄ-RⓄ

this questo KWⓔS-TⓄ

thread filo FⒺⒺ-LⓄ

throat gola GⓄ-Lⓐ

Thursday giovedì JⓄ-Vⓔ-DⒺⒺ

ticket biglietto BⒺⒺL-Yⓔ-TⓄ

tie cravatta KRⓐ-Vⓐ T-Tⓐ

time ora Ⓞ-Rⓐ

tip (gratuity) mancia Mⓐ N-CHⓐ

tire gomma GⓄM-Mⓐ

tired stanco ST@N-K©

toast pane tostato P@-N® T©S-T@-T©

tobacco tabacco T@-B@K-K©

today oggi ©-J®

toe dito del piede D®-T© D@L P®-®-D®

together insieme ®N-S®-®-M®

toilet toilette / gabinetto

    TW@-L®T / G@-B®-N®T-T©

toilet paper carta igienica K@R-T@ ®-J®-N®-K@

tomato pomodoro P©-M©-D©-R©

tomorrow domani D©-M@-N®

tooth ache mal di denti M@L D® D®N-T®

toothbrush spazzolino da denti

    SP@T-TS©-L®-N© D@ D®N-T®

toothpaste dentifricio D®N-T®-FR®-CH©

toothpick stuzzicadenti ST©©-TS®-K@-D®N-T®

tour giro J®-R©

tourist office ufficio del turismo

    ©©-F®-CH© D@L T©©-R®S-M©

tourist turista T©©-R®S-T@

towel asciugamano @-SH©©-G@-M@-N©

train treno TRⒺ-NⓄ

travel agency agenzia di viaggio
ⓐ-JⒺN-TSⒺ-Yⓐ DⒺ VⒺ-ⓐ-JⓄ

traveler's check traveler's check
TRⓐ-VⒺL-ⒺRS CHⒺK

trip viaggio VⒺ-ⓐ-JⓄ

trousers pantaloni PⓐN-Tⓐ-LⓄ-NⒺ

trout trota TRⓄ-Tⓐ

truth verità VⒺ-RⒺ-Tⓐ

Tuesday martedì Mⓐ̇R-TⒺ-DⒺ

turkey tacchino Tⓐ-KⒺ-NⓄ

U

umbrella ombrello ⓄM-BRⒺL-LⓄ

understand (to) capire Kⓐ-PⒺ-RⒺ

underwear mutande MⓄⓄ-TⓐN-DⒺ

United Kingdom Regno Unito RⒺ-NYⓄ ⓄⓄ-NⒺ-TⓄ

United States Stati Uniti STⓐ-TⒺ ⓄⓄ-NⒺ-TⒺ

university università ⓄⓄ-NⒺ-VⒺR-SⒺ-Tⓐ

up su SⓄⓄ

urgent urgente ⓄⓄR-JⒺN-TⒺ

V

vacancies (accommodation) stanze libere
  STAHN-TSĔ LEE-BĔ-RĔ

vacant libero LEE-BĔ-RO

vacation vacanza VAH-KAHN-TSAH

valuable di valore DEE VAH-LO-RĔ

value valore VAH-LO-RĔ

vanilla vaniglia VAH-NEEL-YAH

veal vitello VEE-TĔL-LO

vegetables verdure VĔR-DOO-RĔ

view vista VEES-TAH

vinegar aceto AH-CHĔ-TO

voyage viaggio VEE-AH-JO

W

wait aspetta AH-SPĔT-AH

waiter cameriere KAH-MĔ-REE-Ĕ-RĔ

waitress cameriera KAH-MĔ-REE-Ĕ-RAH

want, I voglio VOL-YO

wash (to) lavare LAH-VAH-RĔ

watch orologio O-RO-LO-JO

watch out attenzione ⓐT-TⓔN-TSⒺ-ⓄⓃ-Ⓔ

water acqua ⓐⓘ-KWⓐⓗ

water (drinking) acqua potabile

ⓐⓘ-KWⓐⓗ PⓄ-Tⓐⓗ-BⒺ-Lⓔ

we noi Nⓞy

weather tempo TⓔM-PⓄ

Wednesday mercoledì MⒺB-KⓄ-Lⓔ-DⒺ

week settimana SⓔT-TⒺ-Mⓐⓗ-Nⓐⓗ

weekend fine settimana FⒺ-Nⓔ SⓔT-TⒺ-Mⓐⓗ-Nⓐⓗ

welcome benvenuto BⓔN-Vⓔ-Nⓞⓞ-TⓄ

well done ben cotto BⓔN KⓄ-TⓄ

west ovest Ⓞ-VⓔST

what cosa KⓄ-Zⓐⓗ

wheelchair sedia a rotelle

SⓔD-Yⓐⓗ ⓐⓗ BⓄ-TⓔL-LⓄ

when? quando? KWⓐⓗN-DⓄ

where? dove? DⓄ-Vⓔ

which? quale? KWⓐⓗ-Lⓔ

white bianco BⒺ-ⓐⓗN-KⓄ

who? chi? KⒺ

why? perché? PⓔB-Kⓔ

wife moglie MOL-Yẽ

wind vento VẼN-TO

window finestra FEE-NẼS-TRah

wine vino VEE-NO

wine list lista dei vini LEES-Tah DẼ VEE-NEE

winter inverno EEN-VẼR-NO

with con KON

woman donna DON-Nah

wonderful meraviglioso MẼ-Rah-VEEL-YO-SO

world mondo MON-DO

wrong (incorrect) sbagliato SBah-L-Yah-TO

XYZ

year anno ah'N-NO

yellow giallo Jah'L-LO

yes sì SEE

yesterday ieri Yẽ-REE

you tu TOO

zipper cerniera CHẼR-NEE-ẽ-Rah

zoo zoo TSO-O

THANKS!

The nicest thing you can say to anyone in any language is "Thank you." Try some of these languages using the incredible EPLS Vowel Symbol System.

Spanish	French
GR@H´-S(EE)-@HS	M(ER)R-S(EE)

German	Italian
D@H´N-K(UH)	GR@H´T-S(EE)-(E)

Japanese	Chinese
D(O)-M(O)	SH(EE)(E) SH(EE)(E)

Swedish	**Portuguese**
T(ah)K	(O)-BR(EE)-G(ah)-D(O)

Arabic	**Greek**
SH(oo)-KR(ah)N	(ē)F-H(ah)-R(EE)-ST(O)́

Hebrew	**Russian**
T(O)-D(ah)́	SP(ah)-S(EE)-B(ah)

Swahili	**Dutch**
(ah)-S(ah)́N-T(A)	D(ah)NK (oo)

Tagalog	**Hawaiian**
S(ah)-L(ah)-M(ah)́T	M(ah)-H(ah)́-L(O)

INDEX

NOTES

QUICK REFERENCE PAGE

Hello

Buon giorno

BWON JOR-NO

Good-bye

Arrivederci

ah-REE-Vě-DěR-CHEE

How are you?

Come sta?

KO-Mě STah

Fine / Very well

Molto bene

MOL-TO Bě-Ně

Yes

Sí

SEE

No

No

NO

Please

Per favore

PěR Fah-VO-Rě

Thank you

Grazie

GRah-TSEE-ě

I would like...

Vorrei....

VO-Rě-EE...

Where is...

Dov'è...?

DO-Vě...

I don't understand!

Non capisco!

NON Kah-PEE'S-KO

Help!

Aiuto!

ah-Yoo-TO
